# BOUGHTON HOUS[E]

NORTHAMPTONSHIRE HOME OF THE
DUKES OF BUCCLEUCH AND QUEENSBERRY

The Duke and
Duchess of Buccleuch
and Queensberry

West Front of Boughton House, c. 1800

BOUGHTON HOUSE

There are few features of an historic house that leave a more powerful and lingering impression than atmosphere. Over hundreds of years embracing births, marriages and deaths, it is hardly surprising that such emotions as happiness or sorrow, love or hatred should leave their marks, perhaps in metaphysical terms such as colour schemes in decor, the style of paintings and furniture collected, but more usually in a cocktail of abstract sensations that can only be summarized by the word 'atmosphere'.

I, for one, am quite intoxicated by Boughton's atmosphere, which is further enriched by more positively identifiable factors. For instance, a unique blend of fragrances exudes from the panelling, the dust in the tapestries, the smoke from particular oak logs and such seasonal variations from new-mown grass and the great Philadelphus bushes peering through the south windows. To this can be added the mystery sounds, the creaking woodwork, a sudden fall of soot down a chimney, the whistling of wind through ancient window frames, the ticking of clocks and – hopefully, no longer! – the munching of death-watch beetles.

Atmosphere is delicate and fragile. To my senses Boughton's is one of tranquillity and happiness with a timeless quality very much its own. As one who occupies only a fleeting part of its 500-year history, I am happy to share this atmosphere with those who respect it and treat it tenderly.

The Duke of Buccleuch and Queensberry, K.T.

# THE LIVING LANDSCAPE TRUST

**B**oughton is a family home lived in by the Duke and Duchess of Buccleuch and by their eldest son and his wife, the Earl and Countess of Dalkeith, and their children.

It is looked after by an educational charity, the Living Landscape Trust, established by the Duke in 1986. The Trust's purpose is to foster understanding of the House and its heritage and the surrounding Boughton Estate with which it has always been intimately linked. Amongst its priorities is conservation of the extremely fragile structure and contents, and gradual restoration of the outstanding designed landscape.

The Duke and his family are enormously grateful to all those who contribute to this work, be they Trustees or the dedicated staff and craftsmen who devote so much skill and time to it. In particular they pay tribute to the late John Cornforth, the country house historian and writer who was a generous adviser and friend to Boughton over several decades.

*The Earl and Countess of Dalkeith
and their daughter Amabel*

*Dr David Bellamy, a Living Landscape
Trustee, with pupils of Windmill House
School at the Boughton Estate
Open Days for Schools*

# CONTENTS

    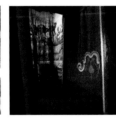 

To help your understanding of this extremely rich and complex building this guidebook is split into three parts:

Section 1 (pp. 9-19) provides an introduction and overview of the history of Boughton, the Montagu family who built it and their descendants, the Montagu Douglas Scotts, Dukes of Buccleuch, who live there now.

Section 2 (pp. 20-74) gives a room-by-room description, tracing the route taken by the majority of visitors. At the end there is a glossary of the artists, craftsmen and terms most frequently mentioned. The large dust-flaps have been designed to act as markers for easier reference.

Section 3 (pp. 75-79) tells of the surrounding landscape and the associated villages and churches where the fine family monuments are to be found.

# A BRIEF HISTORY OF BOUGHTON

Boughton has been the home of the Montagus and their descendants since 1528. It started life as a simple Tudor manor with a Great Hall at its heart, and for 150 years it expanded gently, organically as various courtyards and appendages were added. Then, in two decades of hectic building, the long North Front where the visitor arrives, with its distinctive mansard roof and flavour of Versailles, rose up to embrace State Rooms and Stables. For Ralph Montagu, later 1st Duke of Montagu, a passionate builder and patron of artists, craftsmen and decorators of every sort, this transformation was the pursuit of a dream – to bring French beauty and style to an English landscape.

Magnificent though Boughton appears today, his original vision was never completed. One wing remains empty, and new façades on the south and west fronts never materialised. Ralph's son John, the 2nd Duke was more interested in developing the formal garden and landscape that his father had embarked on. In retrospect we can see how fortunate this was. It left a rare amalgam of grandeur at face value and village-like charm and complexity behind, with its plethora of courtyards, staircases, chimney stacks and roof levels.

Ralph inherited Boughton in 1684. John died in 1749. For 64 years activity in the house and park was at its zenith. From the surviving accounts we know that work of some sort was going on almost all the time. Visitors were constantly passing through; the entertaining must have been incessant.

And then it fell silent. John's heir, his daughter Mary, married a neighbour, the Earl of Cardigan at nearby Deene. Their daughter, also an heiress, married a Scottish Duke and his family, the Scotts of Buccleuch, had plenty of houses of their own. So suddenly Boughton was no longer required, let alone centre stage. Thus there was no demand to refashion the house to the latest Victorian enthusiasm, nor by virtue of its 150 years of slumber did much wear out through over-use. Any decay was gradual, inside and outside in particular where the intricate waterways slowly silted up.

Then slowly, at the beginning of the 20th century, Boughton came back into family focus again. Its magic began to cast a spell so that each summer the house would awaken and the Duke and his family, children, cats, dogs and ponies would arrive for a few months. As they did so, they gently restored it bringing with them a wonderful array of treasures to add to those already there.

By then the process of house accumulation was in reverse. Just before the First World War the family's London home at Montagu House had been given up and, just after it, the main home at Dalkeith was also emptied. Not only did Montagu possessions return to Boughton, but along with them came many of the important pieces of later French furniture and porcelain collected by Buccleuch Dukes in the 19th century, which found happy echoes in this most French of houses.

And so Boughton is today very much alive, a home, a place of beauty and serenity, a treasure house that opens its doors to visitors as it has done for centuries. The work of conservation and restoration goes on – the return of the State Bed in 2003 a striking symbol of that – whilst outside, the form of its wonderful landscape is gradually re-emerging as the layers accumulated over the centuries are carefully peeled away.

# THE ANCESTRY OF THE MONTAGUS

Interest in genealogy is a growth industry. People are fascinated by their origins and ancestors, encouraged by popular television programmes, computers and the power of the web, with its access to public and parish records.

We can perhaps understand, therefore, the desire 300 years ago of Ralph and John, the first two Dukes of Montagu, to establish their family origins. The more immediate Montagu roots in the 15th century were relatively modest, and they were no doubt hoping to alight upon forebears of note further back, even if it meant drawing on descent through the female line. When they succeeded and then also rose in status themselves, as Horace Walpole noticed, they made sure it was well recorded throughout the House. Coats of arms, monograms and coronets all appear on chimney pieces and painted ceilings, in elaborate marquetry and woven into tapestry and rugs. The research was no doubt painfully time consuming, but in undertaking it they were far from unusual, for among their contemporaries in the 17th and 18th centuries there was much enthusiasm for antiquarian inquiry.

The chart opposite illustrates how they traced the family through William de Montacuto, created Earl of Salisbury, back to the Norman invasion in 1066, when a knight called Drago de Montacuto arrived with the Conqueror. Pursuit of another line brought them descent through Ralph Monthermer, Earl of Gloucester and back to Edward I. Duke Ralph even commissioned posthumous portraits, which today are on display in the Armoury. Attributed to Jeremiah van der Eyden (d.1697), we know from the 1718 inventory that they were hanging in the Great Hall, where they were seen by Walpole, who wrote of several 'imaginary ancestors'.

This ancestry is illustrated in detail in the massive carved stone overmantel of the Little Hall, put in by John, 2nd Duke, who was, if anything, more interested in the subject than his father. It was he who also commissioned the 64 shields that encircle the Audit Room, which remind visitors of the family's descent from Edward I and his Queen, Eleanor, whose coat of arms can be seen at the north end (illustrated opposite, top middle).

Thus it is not surprising that Duke John took particular care in maintaining the Eleanor Cross, which is just beyond the Park Walls in the village of Geddington. After the Queen's death in Nottinghamshire on 28th November 1290, her funeral cortège wove its way south towards Westminster Abbey. At each overnight stop her grieving husband had a memorial cross erected. The one at Geddington, unlike the better known one at Charing Cross, retains the original construction and carving.

Duke John had been made a Knight of the Garter in 1718, thus fulfilling his dream of following in the footsteps of William, 2nd Earl of Salisbury, one of the founding members when the Order was established by Edward III in 1345. He celebrated by commissioning the firebacks that can be seen throughout the house, which show the Garter ribbon and its motto *Honi soit qui mal y pense*, surrounding the three Montagu lozenges and surmounted by a ducal coronet.

*'…there were nothing but pedigrees all round me and under my feet…'*

Horace Walpole, visiting Boughton in 1763

Drago de Montacuto (1040-1125)
Arrived in 1066 with the Norman Conquest

Edward I, King of England = Eleanor of Castile
(1239-1307)                              (1241-90)
Had 14 children
including Joan of Acre

William de Montacuto
1st Earl of Salisbury (1301-44)
and Hereford created Earl of
Salisbury in 1337 and Marshall of
England in 1338. His eldest son, the
2nd Earl, was a founding member of
the Order of the Knights of the
Garter. His second son was
Sir John de Montacute

Ralph de Monthermer, Earl of Gloucester = Joan of Acre
and Hereford (d. 1325)                              (1272-1307)

Thomas de Monthermer
2nd Baron Monthermer (1301-1340)

*Eleanor Cross in Geddington*

*18th century fireback*

Sir John de Montacute = Margaret de Monthermer (1329-1394)

Sir Simon de Montacute = a daughter of William of Houghton
Through his wife Simon inherited
Hanging Houghton in Northamptonshire
and was the first Montagu to live in the
county. Four generations later a direct
decendant married Richard Ladde, who
changed his name to Montagu. Amongst
their children was Thomas Montagu

Thomas Montagu (1452-1517) = Agnes Dudley
Purchased the Manor of Hemington 5 miles from Boughton

Sir Edward Montagu of Boughton
Lord Chief Justice (c. 1490-1557)
Began the process of acquiring Boughton and other lands nearby in 1528

# THE MONTAGUS AT BOUGHTON

## Sir Edward Montagu (c. 1490–1557)

Edward was the second son of Thomas Montagu of Hemington in Northamptonshire. His success in the law enabled him to establish the family's foundations as landed gentry. His acquisition of Boughton in 1528 was followed by that of several nearby manors – Weekley, Warkton, Geddington and also Barnwell to the east – before finally consolidating his estate in the 1540s with the purchase of local property interests that had belonged to St Edmundsbury Abbey. Legal adviser to the Abbot of Peterborough, knighted in 1537, he became Chief Justice of the King's Bench in 1538/9. In 1545 he was made Chief Justice of the Common Pleas and was one of the Commissioners of Henry VIII's will. Rather less fortuitously, he was also involved in the drafting of Edward VI's will which named Lady Jane Grey as successor rather than Queen Mary. It led to a period of imprisonment in the Tower of London. He died in 1557 and is buried in nearby Weekley Church, where the inscription on his tomb reads:

*"Farewell to Edward Montagu father of justice and master of the law, you, whom sober skill has nourished and wicked knaves of men have feared have lived in the ancient manner, a lover of peace an unyielding guardian of virtue and a scourge of vice O venerable ancient, prodigal youth fears you as an avenger of crime and takes joy in your death but bereft of pious cato your country mourns you who lived to be its highest defence of justice and equity - this man, reader (you), as you pass by remember in your prayers"*

## Edward, 1st Lord Montagu (1562-1644)

Like his grandfather, Edward, 1st Lord Montagu was briefly incarcerated in the Tower. He was created Lord Montagu in 1621, a privilege gained as someone 'honest and faithful' to the King but helped, as was customary for the times, by a payment of £10,000. He came from a generation of notable brothers - one was successively Bishop of Winchester and Bishop of Bath, two others founded dynasties of note; Henry's family became the Earls of Manchester (1626) and Sydney's the Earls of Sandwich. Although of a more retiring disposition, he was a generous local philanthropist founding the Montagu Hospital (1611) and the Free School (1624), both in the nearby village of Weekley. He had a powerful sense of morality. One contemporary noted him as being 'so severe and regular in his life that he was by most reckoned amongst the Puritans'. Although critical of Charles I, Montagu remained loyal and it was the Parliamentarians who had him shut in the Tower early in the Civil War. His ill health led to release under house arrest in his home in Whitehall, where he died in 1644. Like his father and grandfather, he is buried in Weekley Church.

Sir Edward Montagu
(c. 1490-1557) ————
= Elenor Roper

┌─ Sir Edward Montagu
(1531-1602) ————
= Elizabeth Harrington

┌─ Edward, 1st Lord Montagu
(1562-1644) ————
= Frances Cotton

# Ralph, 1st Duke of Montagu (1638-1709)

Ralph is the single most significant individual in the story of Boughton. Born a younger son, he had few expectations until his brother Edward died in 1665 fighting at sea against the Dutch. Always driven to succeed and not overburdened with scruples, Ralph got his first foot on the ladder by succeeding Edward as Master of the Horse to Queen Catherine. According to a contemporary he 'daily advanced in favour at Court' and was rewarded with the appointment as Ambassador to Louis XIV in 1666. The first of several appointments to the post - he served again from 1669-72, in 1676 and in 1677-78 - it was to transform his life. He was dazzled by Versailles and won over by the French King, who ordered that the fountains should 'play' whenever he was visiting. What he saw there he dreamt of repeating in England in the houses he was to build for himself – Montagu House in London, and at Boughton – and through his influence on Court taste after he became Master of the Great Wardrobe in 1671. His life was a rollercoaster of fluctuating fortunes, particularly in politics. Living through the reigns of four Kings and Queens – Charles II, James II, William and Mary and Queen Anne – his combination of strong Protestant opinions and pursuit of self-interest meant that he would spend many years abroad – once in self-imposed exile – on the continent. The silver lining to his periods of exile was that he gathered round himself, and brought to join others in England, the most talented decorative artists and craftsmen he could find, many being Dutch, many also French refugees escaping religious persecution, the Protestant Huguenots. Two judicious marriages to women of great fortune – in 1673 to Elizabeth Wriothsley, Countess of Northumberland, and, after her death, to Elizabeth Cavendish, Duchess of Albemarle in 1692 – helped finance his considerable expenses. Created Earl of Montagu in 1689, he probably achieved the coveted Dukedom only as a result of his son's marriage to Mary Churchill, daughter of the great Duke of Marlborough.

The Dukedom came in 1705, just four years before his death. Despite his ultimate lack of success in public life, he was well compensated by the intelligent, creative friends who surrounded him and William Congreve's words of dedication to him in 'The Way of the World', in 1699, reflect their respect:

*'If I am not mistaken, poetry is almost the only art which has not laid claim to Your Lordship's patronage. Architecture and painting, to the great honour of our country have flourished under your influence and protection.'*

Edward, 2nd Lord Montagu
(1616-1684)
= Anne Winwood

Ralph, 1st Duke of Montagu (1638-1709)
= Elizabeth Wriothsley (d.1690)
= Elizabeth Cavendish

## John, 2nd Duke of Montagu (1690-1749)

*by Godfrey Kneller*

Although he appeared to be somewhat in the shadow of his father, Duke John was a man of many parts, who played a valuable role at Boughton, especially in developing the landscape. He was married at the age of 15 to Mary Churchill, daughter of the great Duke of Marlborough, and a military strand ran through his life. As a soldier on active service who rose to the rank of General, and as Master-General of the Ordnance with responsibilities at the Tower of London, he took great interest in technical aspects of weaponry and warfare. In 1722 he even fitted out his own expedition of six ships to take St Lucia and St Vincent in the West Indies, although it proved a failure. Notwithstanding the comments of his mother-in-law, who took exception to his penchant for playing practical jokes in his house and gardens – '*All my son-in-law's talents lie in things only natural in boys of fifteen, and he is about two and fifty*' – he was an enthusiastic antiquarian and historian and the builder of a new family home, Montagu House, overlooking the Thames in Whitehall. His great passion was for extending the Boughton landscape: as well as replanning the water features, he planted many of the miles of avenues that still distinguish the surrounding countryside. Amongst the more curious sides to his character was a love of animals – according to the biographer of his friend William Stukeley, '*he would have no cattle or horses killed but brought to end their days peacefully in a special paddock while he was surrounded by dogs, the ugliest of which he favoured because no one else would be kind to it*'.

## Mary, Duchess of Montagu (1712-1775)
## and George Brudenell, 3rd Duke of Montagu (1712-1790)

*by Thomas Gainsborough*

The 2nd Duke's three sons having died in infancy, the future not only of his estates but of the family name and titles hung in the balance. His elder daughter, Isabella, was judged to have made an unfortunate second marriage, so he committed the bulk of his property to his other daughter, Mary. In 1730 she married their near neighbour at Deene, George Brudenell, 4th Earl of Cardigan, though it was on condition – reinforced later in a private Act of Parliament – that George took the name Montagu. This determination was rewarded in 1766 when the Dukedom of Montagu was re-created for the second and final time. To satisfy the needs of Isabella, the old Montagu House in Bloomsbury was sold in 1754 to become the home of the British Museum. Boughton, however, was the subject of a legal dispute between the sisters. With Deene close at hand, Boughton was left unoccupied, as it was to remain for well over a century. The Duke and Duchess were great collectors, however, frequently travelling on the Continent and sending back several fine Old Masters including the El Greco, as well as various pieces of furniture and bronzes at Boughton today. The Duchess died in 1775 but the 3rd Duke, Governor of Windsor Castle, outlived her to 1790.

John, 2nd Duke of Montagu
(1690-1749)
= Mary Churchill

George Brudenell, 3rd Duke
of Montagu, 1766
= Mary, 2nd dau. of John,
2nd Duke of Montagu

*by Pompeo Batoni*

*by Thomas Gainsborough*

# John, Marquis of Monthermer (1735-70)

# Lady Elizabeth Montagu (1743-1827)

The only son of George, 3rd Duke and Mary, John was a delicate young man, whose death in 1770, while still unmarried, brought an end to any hopes of the ducal title surviving. He had spent many years abroad in the hope of improving his health, accompanied by a tutor, Henry Lyte, who corresponded regularly with his parents about his progress. Five years in France included the study of drawing, mathematics and philosophy, although Lyte regretted his charge's 'perseverance in not talking French'. A further five years in Italy followed as an adventurous and acquisitive Grand Tourist. In January 1755 John was one of the first to travel south of Naples, visiting classical ruins. In 1758 he spent time in Venice and Rome, where he was painted by the two leading classical portraitists of the day, Batoni and Mengs.

John's sister Elizabeth married Henry, 3rd Duke of Buccleuch in 1767 and on her brother's death she became the Montagu heiress.

John, Marquis of Monthermer, 1735-70

Henry, 3rd Duke of Buccleuch and
5th Duke of Queensberry
= Elizabeth, dau.of George,
3rd Duke of Montagu

# THE MONTAGU DOUGLAS SCOTTS AND BOUGHTON

The marriage of Elizabeth Montagu to Henry, 3rd Duke of Buccleuch in 1767 and her inheritance of the estate, was the prelude to a new phase in the history of Boughton. The family she had married into, the Scotts of Buccleuch, had their own proud history stretching back to the 12th century. Their Estates were already extensive. As well as houses in the Scottish Borders such as Bowhill and their principal residence at Dalkeith Palace near Edinburgh, they had a house in Oxfordshire.

The Dukedom had been created when Charles II's son, James, married the heiress Anne Scott in 1663, which brought with it descent both from Mary, Queen of Scots, and Henri IV of France, of whom a bust and portrait can be seen at Boughton. The young couple were created Duke and Duchess of Monmouth and Buccleuch, although the Monmouth title was lost after James's execution in 1685.

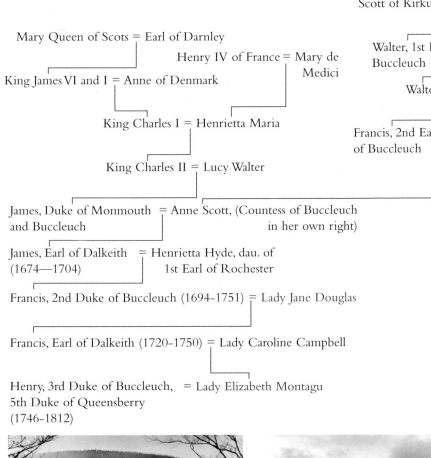

*Drumlanrig Castle*

By curious coincidence Henry, 3rd Duke not only benefited from Elizabeth's inheritance but also succeeded, in 1810, to much of the property and titles of the Douglas', Dukes of Queensberry. In this case the Ducal title was transmitted through the female line, his grandmother, Lady Jane Douglas, being the link. Again, huge estates were added and a great castle, Drumlanrig, in south-west Scotland. Lady Jane was the daughter of James, 2nd Duke of Queensberry, known as the 'Union Duke' for the part he played in uniting the Parliaments of England and Scotland in 1707. The Douglas ancestry can be traced back to the 12th century and includes James Douglas, the great friend of King Robert the Bruce, whose commitment to take the great King's heart on a crusade is commemorated in the family crest. William, 1st Duke of Queensberry built Drumlanrig between 1679-89 and it remains one of the principal seats of the Dukes of Buccleuch. The 4th Duke of Queensberry, known as Old Q, died in 1810 without legitimate heir, and it was at that time the Dukedom and Marquisate went their separate ways.

*Bowhill*

*Dalkeith Palace*

Lady Elizabeth Montagu = Henry, 3rd Duke of Buccleuch,
5th Duke of Queensberry
(1746-1812)

Charles, 4th Duke of Buccleuch = Harriet Townshend,     Five other children
(1722-1819)     dau. of Viscount Sidney     *Including Henry Lord Montagu of Boughton*

Walter Francis, 5th Duke of = Charlotte Anne Thynne,     Six other children
Buccleuch (1806-1884)     dau. of 2nd Marquess of Bath

William, 6th Duke of = Louisa Hamilton, dau. of     Five other children
Buccleuch (1831-1914)     1st Duke of Abercorn     *Including Henry 1st lord Montagu of Beaulieu*

John 7th Duke of Buccleuch = Margaret Bridgeman,     Seven other children
(1864-1935)     dau. of 4th Earl of Bradford

Walter Francis, 5th Duke of Buccleuch was Duke from 1818 to 1884 and contributed enormously to the development of his estates and general rural prosperity. He and his wife, Charlotte Anne, also added greatly to the collections, especially French furniture, porcelain and silver. In 1836 he bought the great painting by Canaletto (now at Bowhill) of Whitehall showing the large courtyard at the back of Montagu House. Later in the century William Burn designed a new house set back from the river. This remained a much-used home for the family until the site was taken back by the Crown in 1917.

John, 7th Duke of Buccleuch and his family began the gradual process of breathing life back into Boughton at the start of the twentieth century. Both his son and grandson – John, 9th, and, present, Duke – supported by their respective wives, have continued the process, showing sensitivity and a deep love of the House. Important conservation projects of recent years have included reinstatement of the pool and fountain in the Fish Court and a large-scale restoration programme for the extensive textile collection.
*Photograph of the 8th Duke and his family entertaining Queen Mary*

Sir David Montagu Douglas Scott was the son of Admiral Lord Charles Scott. Lord Charles had settled in the Dower House next to the Stables in the 1880s and it was there that Sir David lived until his death, aged 99, in 1986. By far the longest lived resident of Boughton, he created a wonderful atmosphere in his house with his own fine and eclectic collections. He developed an outstanding garden with the help of Dorothy, his first wife, and, after her death, his second wife, the renowned gardener Valerie Finnis.

Walter, 8th Duke of Buccleuch = Mary Lascelles,     Seven other children
(1894-1973)     dau. of Major Lascelles     *Including H.R.H. Princess Alice, Duchess of Gloucester*

John, 9th Duke of Buccleuch, = Jane McNeill, dau. of John     Elizabeth = 10th Duke of     Caroline = Lord Gilmour of Craigmillar
11th Duke of Queensberry     McNeill of Colonsay     Northumberland
(b.1923)

Richard, Earl of Dalkeith = Elizabeth Kerr,     John = Berrin Torolsan     Charlotte Anne = Comte Bernard     Damian = Elizabeth Powis
(b.1954)     dau. of the 12th     de Castellane
Marquess of Lothian

Louisa Jane     Walter, Lord Eskdaill     Charles     Amabel     Boniface     Rose     Pierre     Alexander

# BUILDING BOUGHTON

Edward Montagu was in his late thirties when, in 1528, he acquired part of the manor of Boughton from one Robert Burden. He owned land already in Northamptonshire and at least one house at Hemington, but was seeking to consolidate a small estate for himself as his own career and status progressed. Manors at Weekley, Warkton, Geddington and Kettering were acquired, and in 1541 he purchased the remainder of the Boughton manor, which had belonged to the Abbey of St Edmundsbury, 70 miles away in Suffolk.

The park at Boughton had been enclosed in the 1470s and lay on either side of the broad valley of the River Ise, which flows through it from north to south. The site of a medieval village is still discernible near the Stables, although any remaining houses were probably removed at the same time as the enclosure. It is tantalising to speculate on the nature of the buildings acquired by Edward: whether they were the remnants of an old monastic complex or the dwelling of successful Calais wool merchants, as the Burdens and their predecessors were.

It is probable that there was an H-shaped building with a Great Hall at its centre, facing south, and a Great Chamber in the western arm. The evidence of the relatively new science of dendrochronology allows us to date the timber used in the roof beams to between 1510 and 1540. This makes it frustratingly difficult to be sure how much Edward bought and how much he built. The steepness of the roof pitch, which can be seen from the Fish Courtyard, marks it out from the surrounding buildings.

At some stage, probably later in the 16th century, a free-standing block to the south was constructed to create an entrance courtyard, and thereafter the west wing was extended from the Great Hall end to link up and create an enclosure.

Several other courtyards appeared as various outbuildings for kitchens, a laundry and a brew house were added later. It was an evolutionary process that was probably at its most active in the 1630s.

The biggest transformation came after Ralph Montagu inherited the House in 1684. He was then in semi-exile, out of favour with the king, but this did not prevent him embarking on the building works shortly afterwards. We have no certain knowledge of the architect he employed, notwithstanding the mention in Colen Campbell's *Vitruvius Britannicus* (1715) of a Frenchman known as 'Mr Pouget'. Research by the late Gervase Jackson-Stops makes a convincing association with drawings by Daniel Marot.

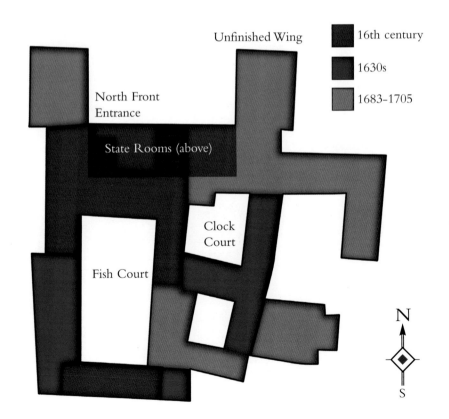

Unfinished Wing

16th century

1630s

1683–1705

North Front Entrance

State Rooms (above)

Clock Court

Fish Court

N

S

A Huguenot refugee designer who worked at Hampton Court for William and Mary, Marot was much patronised by Ralph, particularly for his even more lavish Montagu House in London, which was being rebuilt at the same time following a fire.

The northern protrusions from the H-shape of the Tudor buildings were removed, but otherwise the massive new construction was made to nestle around the old complex. Ralph's intention was to retain the Great Hall, albeit internally remodelled with a barrel vault and painted ceiling, but he was determined to create a formal series of State Rooms, which was the prime purpose of the new North Front. Although strongly French overall, with its mansard roof and the rustication of the stone façades, much of the detailing – the sturdy oak doors, the casement-windowed dormers – is English in character. This is particularly apparent as the visitor penetrates behind the main façade to the series of internal courtyards which give the House its character. After the main block was completed in the 1690s, building work continued with a less ambitious new façade, skin-deep, for the West Front and the completion of the service buildings, which stretched out to the Stables and may not have been finished until 1705.

Apart from the east side of the Stables and the backs of the service buildings, which are in brick, Boughton is built of ashlar stone from Weldon, five miles to the north. Giving particular character to the House are the Collyweston slates on the roofs – nearly two acres in area.

The main entrance to the House is in the north façade through the colonnade, with its nine bays running underneath the State Rooms. What looks like the obvious central doorway is unable to provide a sufficiently distinguished entrance, leading as it does to a dark passage before reaching the Great Hall. Visitors make their way, therefore, beneath the busts of Roman emperors and past the mahogany settees (1728 by George Nix, after designs by William Kent), to the West Door.

*Tudor and French mansard roofs nestling together*

*Watercolour of reconstruction of Great Hall with accurate depiction of existing roof structures by A.W. Blomfield c. 1890*

# The Rooms

# THE LOW PAVILION ANTE-ROOM

For 100 years now this has been the Ante-Room to the Duke's office and that of his secretary, but in Ralph Montagu's time it was the entrance to a group of apartments for important visitors or close members of his family, with the bed chamber beyond.

Ralph's bewigged portrait by Michael Dahl stands out from the religious theme of the other paintings collected over the centuries and brought together by the present Duke. All the furniture, though, was Ralph's and some of it bears the evidence of this provenance. For example, one of the pair of matching mirrors and tables created for him by Gerrit Jensen, c. 1690, includes his interlaced RM initials and the Earl's coronet, which he received in 1689. Opposite, between the windows, the table and matching glass is also by Jensen but, this time, they are japanned and veneered with incised 'Bantam' lacquer; the glass has the later addition of the monogram with the Ducal coronet. The centre table also has a monogram with the letter M and possibly a C to reflect the marriage of Ralph Montagu to his second wife, Elizabeth – born Cavendish – Duchess of Albemarle. It is an interesting piece of wood marquetry that may originally have been a decorative floor panel.

Beneath the painting by Murillo (illustration on previous page) is an exotic writing table (c.1672) created by Pierre Gole, the stylistic precursor to Boulle in France. Its surface is composed of crushed mother of pearl and ebony borders, surrounding pewter on brass marquetry. Now identified as one of a pair made for Louis XIV, it was said, traditionally, to have been gifted by the King to Ralph Montagu during his tenure as English Ambassador in France in the 1670s.

The English chairs, George III, have 18th century needlework covers. Between the rare contemporary Pelletier sconces are four late 16th century alabaster plaques of biblical scenes by Rimbout Tissanaken, Master of Malines.

## PAINTINGS

*Paintings are listed wall by wall, unless otherwise indicated, beginning at the top left of the Fireplace Wall*

Fireplace Wall (north):
*Migration of Jacob.*
Francesco Bassano the Younger (1549-92).

*Madonna & Child with the Infant St John.*
Sebastiano Mainardi (1455-1513).

*The Holy Family with St Catherine.*
Benvenuto Tisi, Il Garofolo
(c. 1481-1559).

East Wall:
*Ralph, 1st Duke of Montagu.*
Michael Dahl (1659-1743).

South Wall:
*Madonna & Child with St John.*
Sébastien Bourdon (1616-71);
floral garland by Mario de'Fiori
(1603-73).

*The Infant St John in The Wilderness.*
Bartolomé Esteban Murillo
(1618-82).

*Rest on the Flight into Egypt.*
Francesco Granacci (1477-1543).

West Wall:
*Christ in the House of Martha & Mary.*
Michel Corneille the Younger
(1642-1708).

# THE STAIRCASE HALL

The view through the windows of the West Front offers a spectacular prospect of the Broad Water and the great avenue of three-hundred-year-old lime trees at the heart of the extensive landscape garden begun by Ralph and greatly extended by his son, John, the 2nd Duke.

Between the windows is a pair of English gilt gesso pier glasses and walnut tables, *c.* 1700. Close by are a set of George III period mahogany chairs decorated with the Scott coat of arms, that of the earlier Dukes of Buccleuch. To the right of the entrance to the Ante-Room is a long-case clock by William Lockin of Rugby, *c.* 1710.

In his vision for the North Front Ralph Montagu must have hoped the central doors of the Colonnade would have worked as a grand entrance into the Great Hall. However, the misalignment of the old and new buildings and the pinched passage space between them must immediately have proved unsatisfactory. The present, apparently side, entrance was therefore adopted as the primary entrance, although this brought its own problems with the difference in levels between the North and West fronts. Such difficulty is masked by the impact of the hall, with its broad staircase, fine contemporary ironwork and the trompe l'oeil decoration of the walls. The matching of the external rustication of the stone with that of the decoration on internal walls was a typical Gallic device. It reflects the approach of Louis Chéron, a Huguenot (French Protestant) artist commissioned by Ralph to paint the ceilings, not just here, but in seven other rooms in the House, including the huge expanse of the Great Hall.

Ralph, like many of his contemporaries, was extremely well educated. He would have been familiar with all the classical allegories illustrated, well versed in the grammar of classical architecture and a cultivated individual, receptive, as a Francophile, to the new and developing fashions he witnessed on the continent. Thus, at first floor level the victorious Roman soldiers with their Dacian captives were taken from reliefs on the Arch of Constantine in Rome. On the ceiling, Mercury is seen holding the Golden Apple thrown by Discord for presentation to 'the fairest Goddess', as he is being despatched by the Gods to find the hapless mortal to undertake the task. His selection of Paris, as judge, triggered the events leading to the legendary Trojan War.

Although it is from a different era, Ralph Montagu would have appreciated the imposing clock half-way up the staircase by Balthazar Martinot of Paris, *c.* 1740. Boldly encased in ormolu by Jacques Caffieri, it sits on a still later gilt-bronze pedestal showing the Goddess Diana, classically revered as a fertility symbol of the city of Ephesus.

*The Caffieri Clock, c. 1740*

# THE HIGH PAVILION ANTE-ROOM

Like its counterpart on the ground floor, the ante-room in this apartment led to a suite of rooms, five in this case, which seems, in Ralph Montagu's time, to have been occupied by distant relatives and close friends, who would often settle in for weeks at a time.

To the right of the door, the portrait of Edward (Ned) Montagu hangs as a reminder that Ralph had been a younger son. Edward died in 1665 during the Second Anglo-Dutch War (1664-1667) while serving with the navy, to which he had turned after being banished from Court. The scandal was recorded by John Evelyn, whose diary reveals that his offence was to 'squeeze' the Queen's hand.

Hanging in the centre of the room is a piece of English crystal, the only contemporary chandelier in the house.

The room contains three examples of important French furniture, the Boulle Cabinet (illustrated above), c. 1700, and the later pair of pedestal cabinets by Etienne Levasseur. These are dated 1775-80 and show the more architectural Neoclassical style in which Boulle marquetry was revived in the Louis XVI period. They were collected by the 5th Duke of Buccleuch and reflect both the enduring family interest in French furniture and the fact that much of the Louis XV and Louis XVI furniture was bought in the 1830s and onwards, when there was again a huge passion for it in England.

*Attributed to André-Charles Boulle, this model of cabinet is a rarity. It has ornate brass scrollwork and mounts on première-partie marquetry of blue-backed tortoiseshell and brass. The masks include Hercules writhing in pain and Daphne with her hair turning into laurel leaves. The cabinet sits on a later English gilt-wood stand.*

*Sir Thomas Tresham (c. 1568), local landowner and a fervent Roman Catholic, whose convictions are evident in the architectural detailing of his intriguing house at Lyveden New Bield and the nearby folly, the Triangular Lodge at Rushton. His son, Francis, died in the Tower for his part in the Gunpowder Plot of 1605.*

## PAINTINGS

Fireplace Wall (north):
*Thomas Howard, Earl of Arundel* (1586-1646). After Daniel Mytens (c. 1590-1648).

*Flower Painting.* Jean Baptiste Monnoyer (1634-99).

*Lady Anne Winwood;* mother of the 1st Duke of Montagu. Attrib. Michiel Jansz van Mierevelt (1567-1641).

*Sir Thomas Tresham* (c. 1545-1605). Dated 1568. English School.

East Wall:
*Prince Maurits of Orange-Nassau* (1567-1625). Michiel Jansz van Mierevelt.

*Sir Ralph Winwood of Ditton* (1565-1617); grandfather to the 1st Duke of Montagu. Attrib. Michiel Jansz van Mierevelt.

*A Surgeon.* Pieter Pourbus (c. 1510-84).

*Edward, 1st Lord Montagu.* English School, 17th century.

*Young Lady, House of Nassau* (?). Attrib. Cornelius de Vos (1585-1651).

*A Surgeon's Wife.* Pieter Pourbus.

*Edward, 1st Lord Montagu.* English School, 17th century.

South Wall:
*Albert, Archduke of Austria* (1559-1621). After Frans Pourbus the Younger (1569-1622).

*A Judge.* English School, 17th century.

*The Hon. Edward (Ned) Montagu* (1636-65). English School.

*Charles V, Holy Roman Emperor* (1500-58). After Titian (c. 1490-1576).

*Wenceslas Hollar in 1657.* Sébastien Bourdon (1616-71).

*Nobleman;* possibly Maximilien de Bethune, duc de Sully (1560-1641). After Frans Pourbus the Younger.

*Prince Rupert, Count Palatine* (1619-82). English School, 17th century.

West Wall:
*Maria Theresa of Austria* (1717-80). Marten van Mytens the Younger (1695-1770).

*Judge;* possibly Sir John Jeffrey, Sergeant-at-Law. English School, 17th century.

*The ebonised, upholstered chairs are William and Mary period and thus contemporary with the fitting out of the room. They have their original coverings.*

L·SERGIVS PAVLVS
ASIAE PROCOS:
CHRTSTIANAM FIDEM
AMPLECTITVR.
SAVLI PREDICATIONE

*The Mortlake tapestry 'Elymas struck by Blindness', from the, c. 1636, Acts of the Apostles set after the paintings by Raphael*

# THE HIGH PAVILION BEDROOM

This large room is dominated by two exceptionally well preserved and vividly coloured tapestries from the Mortlake tapestry factory. They were woven around 1636, during the reign of King Charles I, who purchased the cartoons by Raphael from which they were made. They represent 'Christ's charge to Peter' and 'Elymas struck by Blindness'. Tapestry is particularly vulnerable to being damaged by light, which both fades the colours and weakens the threads. For this reason shutters here and elsewhere in the House are kept permanently closed - sadly excluding the views, to the north and down the West Front avenue, which this pivotal room should enjoy.

Under the 'Elymas' tapestry is a rosewood commode, *c.* 1760, by Pierre Langlois, a French ébéniste with a workshop in Tottenham Court Road. From the same period is the writing table by the Paris-based ébéniste Bernard van Riesen Burgh. Across the corner there is an English gilt gesso dressing table attributed to James Moore. A second pair of the Pelletier glass candle sconces is to be found above the fireplace.

*The decorative paintings that flank the chimney are by the Huguenot Jean Baptiste Monnoyer. Brought to England by Ralph in 1678 he produced a huge number of flower pictures for both Boughton and Montagu House in Bloomsbury – an inventory of the latter in 1707 records 52 of his works. The frames are of equal interest, the upper pair being the work of another of the Pelletier family. The more simple frames, below, are in the style of William Kent.*

## PAINTINGS

Fireplace Wall (south):
*Two Flower Paintings.*
Jean Baptiste Monnoyer (1634-99).

*Thomas Wentworth, Earl of Strafford* (1593-1641). After Sir Anthony van Dyck (1599-1641).

*Two Flower Paintings.*
Jean Baptiste Monnoyer.

*Thomas Brudenell, 1st Earl of Cardigan* (1581-1663); great-great-grandfather of the 3rd Duke of Montagu, himself originally a Brudenell. English School.

West Wall:
*Flower Painting.* Jean Baptiste Monnoyer.

*Anne Churchill, Countess of Sunderland*; the 2nd Duke of Montagu's sister-in-law. After Sir Godfrey Kneller (1646-1723).

*John, 2nd Duke of Montagu.*
Sir Godfrey Kneller, early 17th century.

North Wall:
*Lady Anne Harvey* (1674-1741); daughter of Ralph Montagu. After Sir Godfrey Kneller.

*Charles Talbot, 1st Duke of Shrewsbury.*
Sir Godfrey Kneller, late 17th century.

# THE STATE ROOMS

When King William III arrived at Boughton on October 23rd 1695 the State Rooms, or 'Great Apartment', were barely ready for entertaining the Monarch. The building works, which would have embraced the East Pavilion to match those of the Pavilion rooms on the west, remained incomplete, and it is doubtful how many of the ceilings had been painted. Even the State Bed was somewhat cobbled together from an old French frame, rather than constructed new and in the latest fashion as Ralph would have preferred; time, as so often with big building projects, had run out. Nevertheless, the effect must have been spectacular and, three hundred years on, they remain, perhaps, the most complete survival in an English country house of a series of rooms specially prescribed for the very grandest entertaining.

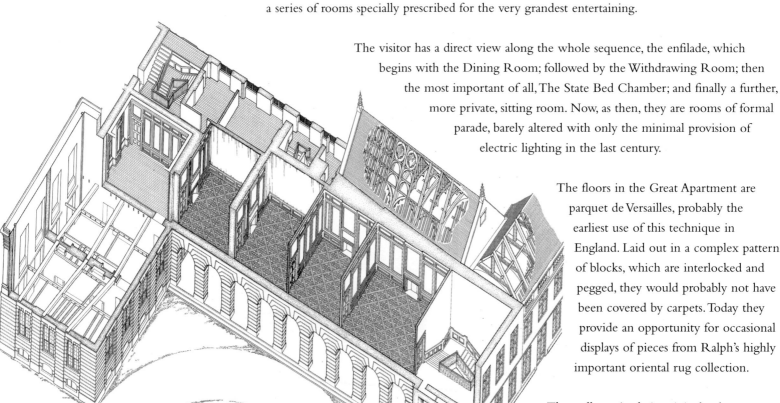

The visitor has a direct view along the whole sequence, the enfilade, which begins with the Dining Room; followed by the Withdrawing Room; then the most important of all, The State Bed Chamber; and finally a further, more private, sitting room. Now, as then, they are rooms of formal parade, barely altered with only the minimal provision of electric lighting in the last century.

The floors in the Great Apartment are parquet de Versailles, probably the earliest use of this technique in England. Laid out in a complex pattern of blocks, which are interlocked and pegged, they would probably not have been covered by carpets. Today they provide an opportunity for occasional displays of pieces from Ralph's highly important oriental rug collection.

The walls retain their original colour, now known in decorating circles as 'Boughton Drab', a variety of khaki shades of great subtlety. The cornices are moulded, not carved, then painted in trompe l'oeil.

As with the ceilings in all these Rooms, the cornices are the work of Louis Chéron. Although under-appreciated, because so little of his work survives elsewhere, and overshadowed by the more prominent artist Verrio, whom Ralph patronised for his London house, Chéron was nonetheless a considerable talent.

The classical allegories, which form the subjects and were no doubt carefully discussed with his patron, often made quite pointed political references. Thus, in the Second State Room the illustration (right), of Ovid's 'Fall of Pyrenaeus' – the tale of a tyrant possessed with an overweening sense of self-worth, seen finally crashing to earth and losing his crown – may well have referred to the flight of King James II in 1688. Ralph Montagu, a firm Protestant, had manoeuvred to push the Bill of Exclusion that would have prevented the Catholic Duke of York from succeeding his brother Charles II, but paid the price of its failure with a period of discreet exile on the Continent. Ralph was, in every way, a beneficiary of the Glorious Revolution which brought William to the throne and the indirect allusion to such events would have pleased both men.

From inventories made in 1697, and shortly after Ralph Montagu died, we know that several of the walls in the State Rooms were covered with tapestries from the Acts of the Apostles sets woven in the Mortlake tapestry factory. The designs painted by Raphael had been commissioned in 1515 by Pope Leo X for tapestries to hang on the lower walls of the Sistine Chapel and formed part of the huge art collection acquired a century later by Charles I. Still part of the Royal Collection, the original cartoons may be seen hanging at the Victoria and Albert Museum, alongside a tapestry from Boughton, which is also on loan to the museum.

Boughton has two different sets based on this design. One, pieces of which can be seen in the High Pavilion Bedroom and the Fifth State Room, was produced in the 1630s by Flemish weavers specially imported to undertake the work. It is of relatively superior craftsmanship to the later second set, pieces of which can be seen in the Second and Third State Rooms, which was woven in the 1670s by English weavers.

*The Mortlake tapestry mark*

Ralph had strong family connections with Mortlake and may have been proprietor for a time, but Boughton's huge tapestry collection - there are over 100 pieces - was drawn from many different manufacturers and designers. Moreover, his position as Mastership of the Wardrobe - a position Ralph acquired for himself and passed on to his son - made him responsible for furnishing the Royal Palaces, so that his patronage was widely spread. He cultivated many English, Dutch, French and especially Huguenot artists and craftsmen, including influential designers such as Daniel Marot and gilders like the Pelletiers - too many to mention - can be found throughout the State Rooms. Even if embryonic at the time of the King's visit, Ralph's vision must have provided the two men with much to discuss and enjoy.

# FIRST STATE ROOM

The First State Room served as the King's Dining Room with tables being brought in and set up for each meal by the servants.

Dominating the scene are two monumental tapestry cartoons purchased by Ralph Montagu. They are identified as the work of Giovanni Francesco Penni, a pupil of Raphael's and a leading member of his workshop. They were executed in charcoal and gouache on paper segments in about 1526. Accounts for the frames are in the archives and show that they were installed in this room in 1722, where they have remained ever since. A fragment of a third, 'The Heads of Men', above the doorway, is attributed to Parmigianino. These modelli – literally models – were used by the weavers to transfer the drawings to their own medium.

The ceiling by Chéron portrays 'Venus Interceding for Aeneas'. Beside the entrance door is a 17th century Boulle encased clock.

The tables and mirrors are set deliberately between the windows in an arrangement that allowed a person's reflection to be seen more clearly during the day.

Above the fireplace is part of the blanc de chine porcelain set, given as a wedding present by the second Duke's robust mother-in-law Sarah Jennings, wife of John Churchill, 1st Duke of Marlborough, the great general and victor of Blenheim.

On the floor, the 'Buccleuch Sanguszko' is one of the most magnificent Safavid rugs in Britain today. Woven in wool in what is known as the 'vase' technique, it dates from the first half of the 17th century; mounted hawkers and fighting dragons can be seen among its palmettes and floral sprays.

## PAINTINGS

Fireplace Wall (south):
*Flower Painting.*
Jean Baptiste Monnoyer (1634-99).

*Anne Savage*; wife of Robert Brudenell, great-grandfather of the 3rd Duke of Montagu. English School, late 17th century.

*Madonna & Child.* Domenico Puligo (1492-1527).

*Elizabeth Stuart, Queen of Bohemia* (1596-1662); elder sister of Charles I. After Paul van Somer (1576-1621).

*Madonna & Child with St John.* Sir Anthony van Dyck (1599-1641).

*Angelica & Medoro with Cupid. c.* 1600. Lorenzo Pasinelli (1629-1700).

Unknown Lady. Cornelius Jonson (1593-1661).

*Flower Painting.*
Jean Baptiste Monnoyer.

*Frances Savile, Lady Brudenell*; married Francis, grandfather of the 3rd Duke of Montagu. After Sir Peter Lely (1618-80).

West Wall:
*Meeting of the Two Holy Families. c.* 1526. Attrib. Giovanni Francesco Penni (1498-1528).

Unknown Lady.
After Andrea Celesti (1637-1712).

East Wall:
*Heads of Roman Men.* 'Parmigianino' (1503-40).

*The Vision of Ezekiel.*
*c.* 1526. Attrib. Giovanni Francesco Penni.

# SECOND STATE ROOM

The tapestries are part of the later Acts of the Apostles set and represent 'The Death of Ananias' (left wall) and 'The Sacrifice at Lystra' (right wall).

The contemporary walnut chairs are covered in crimson velvet. Now much faded, they nevertheless show the way in which the tones of the tapestries and other fabrics would have harmonised. The chairs and materials would have become increasingly lavish as visitors progressed towards the State Bed Chamber. Simple chairs with rush seats and plain damask cushions in the Dining Room give way to velvet and gold brocaded damask to match the luxurious Italian crimson silk of the bed.

The ceiling by Chéron depicts the 'Fall of Pyranaeus'. A portrait by Sir Peter Lely of Ralph Montagu's first wife, Elizabeth Wriothesley, can be seen above the entrance door. Above the fireplace is a masterpiece by Eustasche Le Sueur of 'The Martyrdom of St Lawrence' (1648), painted for the chapel of Saint-Germain-l' Auxerrois. One of the artist's most celebrated works, it was acquired by George, 3rd Duke of Montagu.

*The central table with its monogram is by Jean Pelletier c. 1690.*

*The pier glass, torchères and walnut side table of marquetry and gilt between the windows are all by the French craftsman and designer Daniel Marot.*

## PAINTINGS

Fireplace Wall (south):
*Madonna & Child with St Jerome.*
Leandro Bassano (1557-1622).

*Descent of the Holy Ghost.*
Carlo Dolci (1616-86).

*Martyrdom of St Lawrence.*
Dated 1645-48.
Eustache Le Sueur (1616-55).

*Mystic Marriage of St Catherine.*
Francesco Solimena (1657-1747).

*Holy Family with St John.*
Carlo Maratta (1625-1713).

West Wall:
*Elizabeth Wriothesley* when *Countess of Montagu* (1645-90); Duke Ralph's first wife. *c.* 1689. After Sir Peter Lely (1618-80).

East Wall:
*Queen Mary* (1662-94); painted before her accession to the throne.
Willem Wissing (1656-87).

*The giltwood and gesso chest is by James Moore the Elder (1719).*

# THIRD STATE ROOM

The climax of the State Room series was the State Bed Chamber, a room of formality and ceremony where those privileged would be afforded the 'honour' of witnessing the King's toilette after he rose.

The Boughton State Bed was given by the present Duke's grandfather to the Victoria and Albert Museum in 1918. After an interval of nearly 90 years and having benefited latterly from over 6000 man-hours of painstaking restoration, it has been loaned back, to take its rightful place once again. The richness of its crimson damask hangings with gold brocading and the flamboyance of its original silvered ostrich and egret-feathered finials remind us of the breathtaking boldness of these rooms when new and as originally conceived. The tapestries, from the later set of the Acts of the Apostles, are 'The Miraculous Draught of Fishes', 'St Paul Preaching' and the 'Healing of the Lame Man'.

A mirror of Portuguese ebony and marquetry table by Daniel Marot can be seen between the windows.

The allegory of infidelity in the ceiling painting is of 'Vulcan Catching Mars & Venus in His Net'. Chéron has introduced a particularly clever artistic trick: as the spectator moves through the room, Venus can be seen to 'sit-up' from her initially recumbent position, another variant on trompe l'oeil.

## PAINTINGS

Fireplace Wall (east):
*Elizabeth Percy, Lady Ogle*, later Duchess of Somerset (1667-1722); Duke Ralph's stepdaughter.
Benedetto Gennari (1633-1715).

*James, Duke of Hamilton* (1606-49).
After Sir Anthony van Dyck (1599-1641).

*Lady Frances Seymour, Countess of Southampton* (d. 1681); stepmother of Elizabeth Wriothesley.
After Sir Anthony van Dyck.

Unknown Gentleman.
After Bartel Bruyn the Younger (c. 1550-1610).

*Edward VI* (1537-53).
English School.

*Charles II as a Boy.* Late 1630s.
After Sir Anthony van Dyck.

West Wall:
*Thomas Brudenell, 1st Earl of Cardigan* (1581?-1663). English School.

*Robert Brudenell, 2nd Earl of Cardigan* (1607-1703). English School.

*Edward VI.*
English School, 16th century.

*John, 2nd Duke of Montagu.*
Michael Dahl (1659-1743).

# FOURTH STATE ROOM

**B**y comparison with the Second State Room, the formal Withdrawing Room – the Fourth State Room – was a more private retreat for the King, away from the scrutiny of his courtly circle.

The early inventories refer to this as 'The Blue Room' and it seems likely that blue damask with gold tassels was used for the wall hangings and curtains, in contrast to the crimson and tapestries of the previous rooms. A flavour of this scheme can be seen on the armchair and stool now in the Fifth State Room.

For many years, however, the room has contained French tapestries depicting the story of Gombaut and Macée. This traditional pastoral narrative is told here in a series of tapestries with, on the left, 'The Betrothal' of the eponymous characters. Seven of the original eight pieces are at Boughton, the only near-complete set of this theme to survive; they date from c. 1650-60.

The eye-catching 'flame-stitch' coverings of the contemporary William and Mary period sofas and chairs harmonise relatively well. The pattern is described sometimes as Hungarian, sometimes as Florentine.

On the floor is one of the fine silk Persian carpets of a style commonly, if inaccurately, known as 'Polonaise' (Polish), because although woven in the Middle East, the rugs were imported into Europe through the court in Poland.

The ceiling portrays 'Jupiter restraining Arcas from shooting at the Bear'. According to Ovid, both Arcas and Callisto, his mother, were consequently set among the constellations, Callisto becoming the 'Great Bear'. Unlike other rooms the painted architrave features the "RM" monogram of Ralph Montagu.

## PAINTINGS

Fireplace Wall (east):
*General Daniel Harvey* (1664-1732); husband of Lady Anne Harvey, daughter of the 1st Duke of Montagu.
After Sir Godfrey Kneller (1646-1723).

*Hortense Mancini, Duchesse Mazarin* (1646-99); niece of Cardinal Mazarin and, after 1675, mistress of Charles II. Also friend of Ralph Montagu.
Benedetto Gennari (1633-1715).

*Mary of Modena* (1658-1718).
After Sir Peter Lely (1618-80).

*Lady Anne Harvey* (1674-1741).
Charles Jervas (c. 1675-1739).

*Mary Scott* (1647-61); elder sister (died in adolescence) of Anne, later Duchess of Buccleuch.
After Sir Anthony van Dyck (1599-1641).

West Wall:
*Lady Anne Harvey.*
Charles Jervas, early 18th century.

*An intricately decorated long-case clock by Boulle, c. 1690-5; its centre is bulbous to accommodate the original pendulum – a novelty for a French clock of this period. The glass panel through which the pendulum might have been seen is replaced by one with Ralph's initial, 'M', and his ducal coronet.*

# PAINTINGS

Fireplace Wall (west):
*Sir William Drury* (1527-79).
Attrib. George Gower (1540-96).

The first *Sir Edward Montagu*.
English School, mid-16th century.

*Lady Anne Crouch* (d. 1648);
third wife of Edward, 1st Lord
Montagu. English School.

East Wall:
Unknown Lady.
English School, 17th century.

Unknown Man.
After Cornelis Ketel (1548-1616).

South Wall:
The second *Sir Edward Montagu*
(1531-1602). Dated 1591.
Progenitor of the Earls of
Manchester and Sandwich, as well
as father of the 1st Lord Montagu
of Boughton. English School.

# FIFTH STATE ROOM

At the east end of the Great Apartment, the Fifth Stateroom differs from the others with its plain, boarded floor. It was intended originally to form part of a staircase leading to the upper suite in the East Pavilion, the closed door to which is visible on the north wall.

The 'Death of Sapphira' is from the Charles I set of the Acts of The Apostles tapestries. Sapphira and her husband suffered divine retribution for their meanness towards their early Christian brothers. The tapestry opposite, from the Gombaut and Macée series, shows the two protagonists absorbed in a game of croquet or golf.

Upholstered in the blue damask that may well have been a feature of the previous room are a large armchair and stool, while the remaining giltwood chairs and winged settee are also William and Mary period, though with later coverings.

Above, the ceiling shows 'Cephalus and Aurora,' a story based on a 16th century play by Gabriello Chiabrera.

The corner fireplace carries more Blanc de Chine and is set at an oblique angle in order to share the chimney with the fireplace of the Fourth State Room.

Beside the fireplace is a portrait of Sir Edward Montagu, who acquired Boughton in 1528. It is one of three of him in the House. Above the door leading into the Armoury Passage is a portrait of his son, the second Sir Edward.

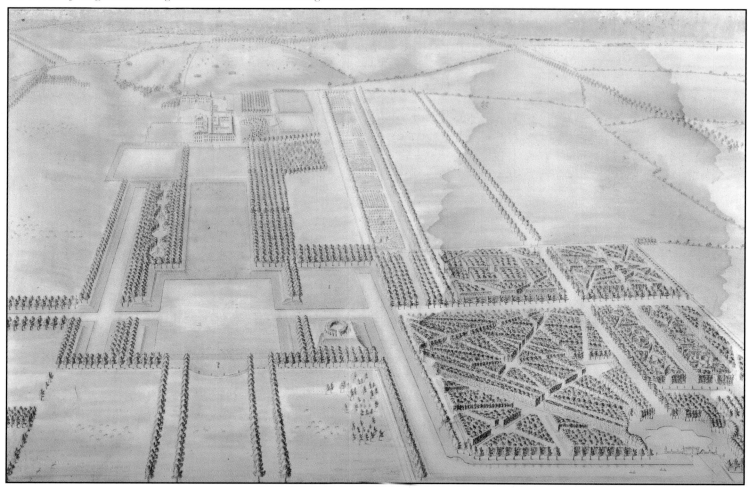

# THE ARMOURY PASSAGE AND LIME STAIRCASE

The immense Boughton armoury collection was housed for many years in rooms along this corridor, hence its name.

The hand-painted maps and plans are of the Montagu estates and date mainly from the 17th and 18th centuries. The plans of the Boughton gardens are particularly valuable, given the accuracy with which they were surveyed and show the evolution of the landscape from the designs of Ralph Montagu's time to the final layout of Duke John. These plans are currently being used to assist the restoration work being undertaken in the Park.

Two other former homes of the Montagu family, Barnwell – not far away at Oundle – and Montagu House in Bloomsbury, London, can be seen in the collection of engravings of notable historic houses.

The Lime Staircase, part of Ralph's 1690s' addition, suffered heavily from woodworm and was carefully restored in the 1950s by estate craftsmen, Robert Humphrey and Alec Bagshaw, using lime wood grown on the estate.

# THE UNFINISHED WING

The greatest surprise of Boughton, and a rare architectural curiosity, is the Unfinished Wing. Externally this 'pavilion' almost matches its twin on the west side, but with the exception of the attic rooms, whose floor rests above, it was left unfinished. Looking back at the first-floor level of the wall through which one enters, you will see the door which would have led from the Fifth State Room into the never-completed upstairs rooms.

The rooms would have replicated those at the other end of the House providing a suite for a distinguished visitor or resident. The death of Queen Mary from smallpox in December 1694 meant that King William travelled to Boughton alone. Moreover, Ralph's second wife, Elizabeth, the former Duchess of Albemarle, who was famous for imagining herself Empress of China, lived at another Montagu home, Ditton, near Windsor. Perhaps without the pressure of necessity, perhaps through a shortage of funds given the work being undertaken on the rebuilding of Montagu House, Ralph obviously decided that he had other priorities.

As a result, late 17th century construction methods and materials are clearly exposed, providing insights into the approach of the builders of the time. The size and variety of some of the beams is striking, as are the angles they adopt. Another feature that becomes more apparent inside is the incorporation of the rainwater down-pipes within the fabric of the walls so as not to disrupt the harmony of the façade.

The empty space provides a home for a variety of artefacts – busts and other statuary, brought indoors for safe-keeping; braziers; a section of elm piping that fed the waterworks in the park; and some travelling trunks that may perhaps have been used by Duke Ralph on ambassadorial duties.

The Unfinished Wing houses the 'Chinese Pavilion', commissioned by Duke John on November 29th 1745 from Samuel Smith. The Pavilion, made of timber and oilskin, was originally placed on the terrace overlooking the Thames at the second Montagu House in Whitehall, where it appeared in a contemporary riverscape painting by Canaletto. The summer house could be dismantled easily for winter storage, the dragon on the apex being a lynch-pin. The Pavilion remained in regular use until the 1960s, being erected each year on the west lawn at Boughton.

A 'Puckle Gun', with a quick-firing brass revolver purchased for Duke John's expedition in the Caribbean (1718-22).

# THE ARMOURY

O nce a Servants' Hall, located next to the kitchen, this is now home to what many experts regard as one of the finest privately-held armouries in the country. It is an historic collection that owes much to Duke John. Although no longer quite on the scale recorded in his Inventory of 1718, which included nearly 900 muskets and over 300 swords, it still includes a large number of pieces of great rarity and exceptional workmanship.

Among a collection of swords of all sorts - for ceremony, for hunting, for wars - is one of the most treasured family heirlooms, the Sword of Ramillies worn by Duke John's father-in-law, the Duke of Marlborough, at some of his greatest battles. Guns of all shapes and sizes are also to be seen, including an early air gun and the extremely rare 'Puckle' gun, invented by James Puckle in 1718. It is one of the earliest examples of a repeat-firing weapon. The collection includes the largest assembly of guns and pistols by Louis Barbar, the Royal Gunmaker in the first half of the 18th century.

Display cabinets contain the livery and regalia worn by the coachman and footmen on the Montagu State Coach, as well as the elaborate harness for the horses. The coach itself is on display in the Stables.

Several of the large paintings attributed to Jeremiah der Eyden (d.1697) are idealized representations of 13th and 14th century Montagu ancestors.

*John, 2nd Duke of Montagu's interest in weaponry may owe something to his father-in-law, the great Duke of Marlborough whom he accompanied into battle as a soldier. He rose gradually to the position of full General in 1746, having raised his own regiment, 'Montagu's Carabineers', the year before. This would certainly have been encouraged by his appointment as Master General of the Ordnance (1740-9) at the Tower of London (shown behind him in this portrait by Thomas Hudson), which enabled him to procure obsolete stock from that arsenal.*

# PAINTINGS

Fireplace Wall (north):
*Edward, 1st Lord Montagu.*
After Adriaen Hanneman
(*c.* 1603-71).

*Frances Cotton* (1586-1620); second wife
of the 1st Lord Montagu.
Marcus Gheerhaerts the Elder
(1516-*c.* 1604).

The first *Sir Edward Montagu; uniformed as
Chief Justice of the King's bench.*
English School, mid-16th century.

*James Scott, 1st Duke of Monmouth
and Buccleuch* (1649-85).
Attrib. Jan Wyck
(*c.* 1640-1702).

*Queen Elizabeth* (1533-1603).
Dated 1595. Marcus Gheeraerts the
Younger (1561-1636).

*Elizabeth Vernon* (1572-1655);
lady-in-waiting to Queen Elizabeth
and later Countess of Southampton.
English School.

*Henry Wriothesley, 3rd Earl of Southampton*
(1573-1624); husband of Elizabeth Vernon.
John de Critz the Elder (*c.* 1552-1642).

50

# THE GREAT HALL

The Great Hall is the largest room at Boughton and remains the most imposing of spaces, as it must have been since its construction in early Tudor times. The sketch by A.W. Blomfeld done in anticipation of the much needed repairs in 1911, which included the installation of the wainscoting panels, gives an impression of how it must have looked. Hidden above the painted barrel ceiling is the original timber roof structure, with its carved windbraces and quatrefoil patterns. This ceiling, 'The Apotheosis of Hercules' by Chéron, was one of the last to be worked on and remains incomplete. It was commissioned by Ralph Montagu around 1705 after he also had installed the windows, opened through two storeys, and the ducal coat of arms in the western ceiling lunette, with its griffins peering down on the activities below.

To the left of the fireplace wearing his red robes and the chain of office of Chief Justice is the first Montagu to be associated with Boughton, Sir Edward, the purchaser in 1528. On the end wall to the left of Sir Edward's portrait is George, 3rd Duke of Montagu, the last to carry the Montagu title. After his death in 1790 the House passed to the Dukes of Buccleuch through his daughter Elizabeth, whose portrait by Gainsborough is to the left of the main door. Her brother is seen in the portrait - resting on an easel - by Pompeo Batoni. It was painted in Rome, where he

spent a number of years as a result of ill health until his death in 1770 at the age of 35.

Above the panelling is The Four Elements series of tapestries – 'Fire', 'Water', 'Air' and 'Earth' – with central shields showing Ralph Montagu's initials and his Earl's coronet. They are the work of John Vanderbank, Yeoman Arras-maker at Hampton Court, made after designs by Charles Le Brun, the great décor overseer at Versailles. The Boughton tapestries were woven in England in the 1680s, with the exception of 'Fire', for which there is an account dated 1699.

Two matching, Boulle, 'coffres de toilette', which held jewellery and medals, are on either side of the doors to the Fish Court. The wicker-backed chairs are William and Mary period and retain much of their original leather coating. The pier tables flanking the fireplace are attributed to Ince and Mayhew in carved giltwood carrying Sicilian jasper slab, c. 1760. The giltwood side table nearest the piano is by Jean Pelletier, c. 1699, and that on the other side of the door is by Matthias Lock, c. 1745; it bears an 'Indian' head, complete with plumed headdress, a motif typical of pattern books of the earlier Louis XIV period.

Hanging between the windows and painting , and bearing the monogram of Charles II, is a set of six silver candle sconces.

East Wall:
*Lady Mary Churchill* (1689-1751); became wife of the 2nd Duke of Montagu. Studio of Sir Godfrey Kneller (1646-1723).

*Sarah Jennings, Duchess of Marlborough* (1660-1744).
Studio of Sir Godfrey Kneller.

*Ralph, 1st Duke of Montagu.*
Benedetto Gennari (1633-1715).

*Elizabeth Wriothesley* when *Lady Montagu.*
Attrib. Pierre Mignard (1612-95).

West Wall (on easel):
*John, Lord Brudenell,* later Marquess of Monthermer; son of the 3rd Duke of Montagu. Dated 1758.
Pompeo Batoni (1708-87).

*Elizabeth Montagu, Duchess of Buccleuch* (1743-1827); daughter of the 3rd Duke of Montagu.
Thomas Gainsborough (1727-88).

*Mary Montagu, Duchess of Montagu* (1712-75); daughter and wife of the 2nd and 3rd Dukes of Montagu respectively. Dated 1767. Thomas Gainsborough.

*George Brudenell, 3rd Duke of Montagu* (1712-90). William Beechy (1753-1839).

*James Scott, 1st Duke of Monmouth and Buccleuch (1649-1685). 1672/3. Jan Wyck (c. 1640-1702) (attrib.).*

*The 18th century silver 'Shell Box of Peruvian Origin' was purchased in 1862 by the great collector, the 5th Duke of Buccleuch; it apparently held coca leaves.*

*Detail from 'Fire' of the Four Elements series. Woven in the 1680s with Ralph Montagu's monogram, there is an account from Vanderbank for £6 for 'putting in' the Earl's coronet in 1695.*

To the right of the fireplace is a portrait of Queen Elizabeth, showing her in the "thirty seventh year of her reign" - 1595. Alongside her are two members of her court, the Earl and Countess of Southampton. Henry, 3rd Earl of Southampton was the great patron of William Shakespeare and his clandestine marriage to the Queen's lady-in-waiting, Elizabeth Vernon, was not approved of by Elizabeth. However, his subsequent confinement in the Tower, seen here in the background, was due to his involvement in the Earl of Essex's uprising of 1601. Elizabeth Vernon, in this unusual portrait, is seen at her 'toilette' with her garments and jewels arrayed around her. The Southamptons were Ralph Montagu's wife's grandparents and through them he inherited property at Beaulieu in Hampshire.

# THE EGYPTIAN HALL

While the Great Hall was no doubt used for large gatherings, the room known as 'The Egyptian Hall' appears regularly in older plans and inventories as being the family dining room. One of the oldest parts of the Tudor house, it was given its painted ceiling during Ralph Montagu's alterations.

Appropriately, the ceiling shows the 'Triumph of Bacchus and Ariadne' who can be seen drawn by leopards and goats in their respective gold and silver chariots surrounded by companions who include the drunken Silenus, riding on his Ass.

The room's curious name refers to an antiquities club known as the 'Egyptian Society', formed in the 1740s and chaired by Lord Sandwich, a cousin of the 2nd Duke of Montagu. The club would sometimes hold its meetings and dinners here, hosted by the Duke and under the auspices of Sandwich and one their great friends, the antiquarian, the Rev William Stukeley. William Stukeley drew plans in 1744 for a 'Gothic' bridge, inspired, perhaps, by the Eleanor Cross (p11). It was to span the canalised River Ise as it passes through the park. Although it apparently took the Duke's fancy, he never got further than asking his joiner Thomas Eyres to build the model.

*'The Adoration of the Shepherds' (c. 1574/5) by El Greco (Domenikos Theotocopoulos) is an early work painted before his arrival at the Spanish Court. It was bought in 1756 by the third Duke of Montagu and at that time was attributed to the Venetian master Tintoretto. However, the shadowy atmosphere and already attenuated figures, and the dramatic plunge into depth created by the entourage of the Magi in the background reveal the true artist's more mannerist predilections.*

# THE AUDIT ROOM

The 84-foot-long Audit Room was formed out of the Steward's Hall and a passage way, sometime between 1720 and 1740. The name suggests it was here that tenants came to pay their rents and where they might traditionally be entertained. A pewter plate, with the Montagu griffin crest on one side, has, etched on the reverse, a record of one such meal: 'Chas Panther used me at Lady Day Audit 1799 and did very well indeed'.

*One of two Sèvres pot-pourri vases, c. 1759, decorated with scenes after David Teniers*

The floor was re-laid in 1952 with oak grown at Boughton. In the two 19th century faux-Boulle cabinets and the display case on the end wall can be seen part of the remarkable Vincennes and Sèvres porcelain collection amassed by Walter Francis, 5th Duke of Buccleuch and his wife, Charlotte Anne. Collected in the 1830s with the help of the dealer E.H. Baldock in a period of barely 18 months, it includes over 100 pieces from Louis XV's own dining set, ordered in 1751 for Versailles. Beautifully painted, and richly edged with gold leaf, the striking turquoise bleu lapis backgrounds immediately catches the eye.

The chimney-piece bears the coat of arms of the first Sir Edward Montagu and must therefore have been removed from another Montagu house. There are two curious inscriptions, one in Latin – NE SIS ARGUS FORIS ET DOMIT ALPA - which translates as 'Do not be a mole at home and a peacock abroad'; the other in French - MILLE DOULEURS POUR UNG PLESURE – which means 'a thousand sorrows for one pleasure'. As with the imaginary ancestors in the Armoury, the 62 heraldic shields round the walls trace the Montagu family descent, ostensibly from Edward I.

Down the centre of the room is a long shovel-board games table. We have the account for its manufacture in 1702/3 for £3.17s.4d. and know it was the work of Roger Davis, the principal joiner involved in much of the panelling and woodwork required by Ralph's building programme.

The English walnut armchairs, c. 1625, have their original velvet covers, which have faded from red to green.

*A Sèvres plate*

## PAINTINGS

Fireplace Wall (east):
*John, 2nd Duke of Montagu.* Thomas Hudson (1701-72).

*Mary Churchill* (with her page, 'Charles'); wife of the 2nd Duke of Montagu. Enoch Seeman (1694-1744).

*John Churchill, 1st Duke of Marlborough* (1650-1722); father-in-law of the 2nd Duke of Montagu. Sir Godfrey Kneller (1646-1723).

*Mary Montagu, Duchess of Montagu* (1712-75); daughter of the 2nd Duke of Montagu. Jeremiah Davidson (c. 1695-1745).

*Ralph, 1st Duke of Montagu.* John Closterman (c. 1660-1711).

*Elizabeth Wriothesley,* when *Countess of Northumberland.* Late 1660s. Sir Peter Lely (1618-80).

*Countess of Shrewsbury* (?). Sir Anthony van Dyck (1599-1641).

*Master Ralph Montagu* (1679-87); oldest child of the 1st Duke of Montagu; died young. John Riley (1646-91) & John Closterman.

A young *Lady Elizabeth Percy;* 1st Duke's stepdaughter. Dated 1670. Sir Peter Lely.

*Lady Frances Brudenell, Countess of Newburgh;* aunt of the 3rd Duke of Montagu. c. 1694. Sir Godfrey Kneller.

*Lady Anna Maria Brudenell, Countess of Shrewsbury;* aunt of the above. c. 1670. Sir Peter Lely.

*Lady Dorothy Brudenell, Countess of Westmorland;* sister of Frances, above. Late 1660s. Sir Peter Lely.

South Wall:
*Wooded landscape with a peasant and his dog.* Jacques D'Arthois (c. 1613-86).

West Wall:
*Algernon Capel, 2nd Earl of Essex* (9th creation) (1670-1710); nephew, by marriage, of Elizabeth Wriothesley. Attrib. Sir Peter Lely.

*Edward, 2nd Lord Montagu* (?) (1616-84); father of the 1st Duke of Montagu. Robert Walker (c. 1600-58).

*General Edward Montagu* (d.1738); brother of the 1st Earl of Halifax. Michael Dahl (1659-1743).

*George Montagu* (1713-80); son of the above. Jean-Baptiste van Loo (1684-1745).

*George Montagu, 1st Earl of Halifax* (1684-1739) (second creation); cousin of the 2nd Duke of Montagu. Michael Dahl.

*Henry, 3rd Duke of Buccleuch* (1746-1812). Katherine Read (1723-78).

*The banners woven in 1705 for the 2nd Duke's wedding are now too fragile for regular display.*

# THE SOUTH PASSAGE

*View of the Thames showing Montagu House by Samuel Scott*

In Tudor times the south wing of the House was a separate building and it was probably not until around 1630 that it was joined up with the cross-wings of the Great Hall to form what we now know as Fish Court. At one time, according to early 18th century plans, it was labelled 'Chappel' Court, suggesting that a chapel may once have been embraced within the south range, though no trace of it remains today.

The South Passage offers an excellent view back to the Great Hall, the original building at the heart of Boughton, with its steeply-pitched roof. The windows were greatly enlarged by Ralph Montagu and an impression of the original Tudor design can be seen in the stone mullioned windows on the upper floor to the left of the Hall.

The paintings on display can vary but will usually include works by 17th century Dutch and other European artists, which are well represented in the Buccleuch Collection. Often hung here is a fine 'View of the Thames' by Samuel Scott showing the Montagu House built for Duke John during the 1730s by Henry Flitcroft. It shows the riverside terrace for which the Chinese Pavilion was ordered.

Upon leaving the passage, one is flanked by 4 pastoral paintings by Francesco Zuccarelli, whilst above the doorway is a portrait, made in 1734, of George Brudenell, later 3rd Duke of Montagu, in the uniform of a Hungarian hussar – a popular masquerade costume of the period.

# THE RAINBOW ROOM

In the late 19th and early 20th centuries this was a dining room but today is primarily a room for display due to the fragility of many of the contents, not least the early 16th century Isfahan carpet.

Two quite different styles of Boulle writing desk can be seen. At either end a pair of kneehole desks with red-backed tortoiseshell and brass marquetry date from early in the Louis XIV period. Compact and almost fussy, they compare with the later more elegant bureau plat in the centre that is the work of André Charles Boulle himself, dating from around 1710.

The console tables with their marble tops supported by giltwood dolphins, *c.* 1740, are attributed to the decorative teamwork of Henry Flitcroft and Benjamin Goodison.

The chairs, William and Mary period, either side of the fireplace have their original and rare green velvet covers. The Boulle encased clock is by Jacques Gloria of Rouen.

The tapestries with their bacchanalian scenes of young boys playing amidst fountains and grapes are Flemish, *c.* 1665. The intertwined spotted snakes that form the borders symbolise immortality.

The drawing on the right of Mary Lascelles, wife of the 8th Duke of Buccleuch and the present Duke's mother, is by her sister-in-law, Molly Bishop (Lady George Scott). On the left is Margaret Bridgeman, wife of John, 7th Duke of Buccleuch by Ellis Roberts; it is a sketch for a portrait at Bowhill.

*One of two Meissen swans by J. J. Kaendler with stands by J-C. Duplessis, commissioned, c. 1750, by Madame de Pompadour*

## PAINTINGS

Upon easels:
Portrait of *Marie Antoinette* (1755-95).
Nicolas Lavreince the Younger (1737-1807).

*Margaret Bridgeman;* wife of the 7th Duke of Buccleuch. Ellis Roberts (1860-1930).

*Mary Lascelles;* wife of the 8th Duke of Buccleuch. Molly Bishop; sister-in-law of the sitter.

Over the doorway:
*Flower Painting.*
Jean Baptiste Monnoyer (1634-99).

Centre Portrait upon Boulle table:
*Louis XIV.* Claude Lefèbvre (*c.* 1637-1675).

# THE MORNING ROOM

The rather alarming display between the Rainbow and Morning Rooms illustrates starkly the damage done by death-watch beetle to the floors of the adjacent rooms. They were replaced in 1976 by our own craftsmen, using oak that had been growing on the Estate for over 300 years.

Although the tapestries of the Morning Room show bacchanalian scenes reminiscent of those in the Rainbow Room, these come from one of two sets in the House known as 'The Naked Boys'. Woven at Mortlake in the 1670s, they feature the 'trademark' St George's cross on the right hand margin. One of the boys can be seen misbehaving in a tree beside the door through to the Drawing Room.

The long-case clock is by C. Halsteads of London, *c.* 1690. The bracket clock is by Richard Bockett and is slightly later in date. Hanging above the clock is a portrait of the young Duke John with his dog; opposite is a portrait of Henrietta Maria Sheldon, one of the 3rd Duke's aunts. Both of these are set in particularly fine frames in the style of William Kent.

The writing table is attributed to Benjamin Goodison, *c.* 1740; the chest of drawers, with bombé front, of about five years later, bears the stamp of the contemporary Parisian ébéniste Antoine Criaerd.

*Wood with
death-watch beetle*

*Sir Anthony van Dyck – self portrait, one of the 40 grisailles on display.*

64

# THE DRAWING ROOM

Once a medieval parlour, then a dining room, the subtly elegant Drawing Room is now firmly centred round the stone fireplace, which was brought here in 1910 from a former Montagu home. Directly in front of the fire is a rug of great historical interest, one of a set of three at Boughton which were once believed to be some of the earliest extant carpets woven in England. They exhibit, at each edge, a coat of arms that includes the Montagu 'lozenges', and woven into the borders of two of them are the dates 1584 and 1585.

Displayed in vertical groupings throughout the room are a set of 40 grisaille portraits by Sir Anthony van Dyck. Painted in oil on oak panels, these were then engraved for his *Iconography*, published in 1645. Van Dyck captured the likeness of leading contemporaries in England and the Netherlands, including his patron Charles I and his friend Peter Paul Rubens. The portraits belonged to Van Dyck's successor as principal Court painter, Sir Peter Lely, from whose posthumous sale in 1682, Ralph Montagu acquired them.

The writing table by Joseph Baumhauer, c.1760, incorporates 24 small square Sèvres plaques mounted round its edge, a concept introduced by S-P Poirier in 1758. The practice of combining porcelain and furniture was further refined by makers including Martin Carlin, whose small writing desk or bonheur-du-jour, nearby, is dated 1768. The desk, with its 17 beautifully painted Sèvres plaques mounted here in 10 irregular shapes, shows how far this fashion in furniture had moved in the century since its inception under Louis XIV and Pierre Gole.

Daniel Marot is credited with the design of the pair of bucolic mirrors fitted with sconces to hold flower vases or candlesticks, although they are thought to have been made and gilded by Jean Pelletier in 1691 for Ralph Montagu. The sofas and chairs are Louis XV period, some of them bearing the stamp of J.J. Pothier.

*The pair of exotic white, 17th century Japanned 'India Cabinets' is recorded as being in Ralph Montagu's bedroom in the mid-1690s. The stands of giltwood are in the manner of James Moore.*

# THE LITTLE HALL

The Little Hall is today the hub of the House, the crossroads where people gather when the family is at home and when guests arrive. It is hard to imagine this room as it once was in the original Tudor building, when, with the adjoining room and at first floor level, it formed the Great Chamber, which had a floor area larger than the Great Hall. Ralph Montagu installed the gallery in 1694 and later had Chéron decorate the painted ceiling, with his interpretation of 'The Return of Proserpine.'

Featured both on the overmantel, as a bronze bust, and riding a white horse in the painting opposite, is Henri IV of France, ancestor of the Dukes of Buccleuch through the marriage of his daughter Henrietta Maria to King Charles I. The first Duke of Buccleuch was James, Duke of Monmouth, their grandson, whose portrait can be seen to the right above the bust. To his left is his wife Anne, the heiress of the Buccleuch lands. On their marriage in 1663 Monmouth's father, King Charles II, who can be seen opposite across the Little Hall, elevated the couple to Duke and Duchess of Monmouth and Buccleuch.

Beside Charles II is a second distinguished portrait of the last of the male Montagus, John, Marquis of Monthermer. Painted in Rome, it is by Anton Raphael Mengs, and shows a more studious, sober image than Batoni's youthful portrait with mandolin, in the Great Hall.

To the left of the fireplace is a bust of the present Duke, a commission to mark his 21st birthday from the artist Oscar Neyman.

The furniture includes the French roll-top desk from 1755-60 and a slightly later pair of dwarf cabinets after Etienne Levasseur, similar to those in the High Pavilion Ante-Room.

In the 'Harvest Scene' David Teniers the Younger portrays himself directing the farm foremen, while his family stand by. Teniers' house, Drie Tueren, is in the background with Het Steen, the home of Rubens, shown in the distance to the right. The 'Hunting Scene' is by John Wootton, but with figures, it has recently been suggested, by William Hogarth. The horseman removing his jacket is John, 2nd Duke of Montagu. Annibale Carracci's, 'Young Man in a Plumed Hat', *c.* 1584, displays the Bolognese painter's increasing grasp of Venetian light and brushwork, a virtuoso display of skill that ultimately bears some of the seeds of early Baroque art.

*Montagu griffins and lozenges on the stone overmantel*

Henri IV of France.
Late 16th century.
French School.

## PAINTINGS

Fireplace Wall (north):
*Flower Painting* (as above each door).
Jean Baptiste Monnoyer (1634-99).

*Edward VI* (1537-53).
After Gwillelm Stretes (fl. 1537-53).

*Young Man in a Plumed Hat. c.* 1585.
Annibale Carracci (1560-1609).

East Wall:
*A Hunting Scene.*
Dated 1730s.
John Wootton (*c.* 1682-1764);
figures by William Hogarth (1697-1764).

*Harvest Scene;* with Château Drie Tueren,
the artist's home.
David Teniers the Younger (1610-90).

South Wall:
*Ferdinand, Duke of Alba* (1508-82).
Attrib. Girolamo da Carpi (1501-56).

*Henri IV of France.* French School,
late 16th century.

*A Child in Leading Strings;*
possibly a segment of a larger painting.
Pantoja de la Cruz (1553-1608).

*A Hunting Scene. John Wootton; figures by
William Hogarth (1697-1764).*

*Harvest Scene; with Château
Drie Tueren, the artist's home.
David Teniers the Younger.*

*Young Man in a
Plumed Hat. c. 1585.
Annibale Carracci.*

West Wall:
*Prince Charles Louis, Elector Palatine*
(1617-80).
After Sir Anthony van Dyck (1599-1641).

*Frederick, King of Bohemia* (1596-1632).
Gerrit van Honthorst (1590-1656).

*Prince Maurice, Count Palatine* (1620-54).
After Sir Anthony van Dyck.

*Elizabeth Stuart, Queen of Bohemia*
(1596-1662). Gerrit van Honthorst.

Upper Gallery
(beginning above Edward VI):
*Anne Scott, Duchess of Monmouth and
Buccleuch* (1651-1732).
Willem Wissing (1656-87).

*James Scott, 1st Duke of Monmouth and
Buccleuch.* Dated 1679.
Sir Godfrey Kneller (1646-1723).

*Mary Churchill, Duchess of Montagu*
(1689-1751).
Charles Jervas (*c.* 1675-1739).

*Children of Charles I: James, Duke of York and
Princess Mary.*
Attrib. John Weesop (fl.*c.* 1641-49).

*John, 2nd Duke of Montagu. c.* 1718.
Charles Jervas.

*Charles II* (1630-85).
*c.* 1675. Studio of Sir Peter Lely (1618-80).

*John, Marquis of Monthermer.* Dated 1758.
Anton Raphael Mengs (1728-79).

BOUGHTON HOUSE

# THE STABLES

The imposing Stable Block was added to the Boughton House complex by Duke Ralph in 1704. The West Front is faced in the same dressed Weldon stone as the main House, whilst the inside archway and the East side is built in rather simpler red brickwork.

Following architects' warnings of imminent collapse in the late 1970s a major five-year restoration work was undertaken. This involved underpinning the foundations, which had been undermined over the centuries by seepage of water from a culvert directly below. The uneven movement of the building has resulted in cracks and distortions that can be seen clearly to the far right of the archway. Steel and concrete frames were inserted in the top of the building to hold it together and, due to the ravages of dry rot, wet rot, death watch beetle and furniture beetle, much of the woodwork has been renewed, using timber from many of the estate elm trees that, sadly, succumbed to Dutch Elm Disease. The interior has been adapted and now houses administrative offices, educational facilities, a tearoom, a gift shop and the exhibition area with the family's magnificent State Coach, built in 1830.

# SOME ARTISTS REPRESENTED AT BOUGHTON

## PAINTERS

FRANCESCO (1549-92) and LEANDRO (1557-1622) BASSANO Brothers from a family of Venetian painters, whose father, Jacopo, was the most accomplished.

POMPEO BATONI (1708-87) Rococo era painter worked in Rome initially on altarpieces for churches and decorative schemes. Famous for his portraits of Grand Tour visitors. Monthermer was painted in 1758.

WILLIAM BEECHY (1753-1839) English portrait painter. Knighted in 1798. Careful and truthful, but lacking at times in spirit. As well as George 3rd Duke, The Buccleuch Collection includes several of his portraits of the Scott family at Bowhill.

SÉBASTIEN BOURDON (1616-71) Born Montpellier, worked in Rome and Venice, then at the Court in Sweden as a Portrait painter. Returned to Paris. Varied output included landscape, genre scenes and religious painting as well as portraits. His nephew, Jacques Parmentier worked for Ralph Montagu in the 1680's.

VINCENZO CAMPI (1530/5-91) Italian living in Cremona. Influenced by Flemish artists like Aertsen and Beuckelaer. Began painting still-life/genre scenes in 1570s. Boughton picture of flower seller previously attributed to Beuckelaer.

ANNIBALE CARRACCI (1560-1609) The greatest of a family of three artists from Bologna where he worked before going to Rome in 1695 to undertake a major commission for ceilings of the Farnese Palace. Boughton portrait of an Unknown Young Man dated c. 1584.

LOUIS CHÉRON (1660-1725) French Huguenot brought to London by Ralph Montagu in about 1693. Recorded as working for him in London, at Ditton and on and off at Boughton on the ceilings for some 12 years. Regularly appears in the accounts, though

£115 was still owing to him at the time of Ralph's death when he is described as a 'history painter'.

MICHAEL DAHL (1659-1743) Swedish. Came to England in 1682 and worked in Kneller's studio. Patronised by Queen Anne.

ANTHONY VAN DYCK (1599-1641) b. Antwerp, trained with Rubens, spent several years in Italy, then back in his native land before settling in England for the last nine years of his life. Hugely influential portrait painter with a large output, quality sometimes diluted by studio assistants. As well as the grisailles there are full-size portraits at Boughton and elsewhere in The Buccleuch Collection.

THOMAS GAINSBOROUGH (1727-88) Born in Suffolk. As well as his landscapes which are some of the most famous icons of English art, he painted outstanding portraits which can be found in many country houses. Never used assistants, even for drapery. He did three portraits of Mary Montagu; a second at Drumlanrig almost identical to that in the Great Hall, and a wonderful three-quarter length to match a similar one of her husband (both 1768 and at Bowhill). Elizabeth was painted at the time of her marriage and Gainsborough also painted her husband, Henry.

MARCUS GHEERAERTS (c. 1520-90) Flemish Huguenot refugee who was in England by 1568. Part of a circle of artists, including John de Critz, his father in law, who were leading portrait painters during Elizabeth's reign. Little documentary or stylistic evidence to assist with attribution and Boughton picture is one of a number of this type.

FRANCESCO GRANACCI (1477-1543) Italian, pupil of Domenico Ghirlandaio.

EL GRECO (Domenikos Theotocopulos) (1541-1614) Born in Crete, came via Italy to settle in Spain where many of his greatest works are to be found. Boughton painting dated c. 1584 but early signs of his distinctive elongated figures and vivid, contrasting, tones are beginning to show.

GERRIT VAN HONTHORST (1590-1656) Dutch, worked in Rome, influenced by Caravaggio. Returned to Utrecht. Court painter at the Hague. Visited England 1628 onwards, painting Charles I, and, as rep. here at Boughton, his sister's family. Elizabeth of Bohemia dated 1634.

THOMAS HUDSON (1701-79) Taught Reynolds but was active himself particularly in 1740s and 50s when the two Montagu Dukes were painted. Also painted 3rd Duke of Queensberry at Drumlanrig.

CHARLES JERVAS (or JARVIS) (c. 1675-1739) Irish. Studied with Kneller, journeyed throughout the Continent but returned to London 1709. As well as aristocratic subjects, painted literary friends including Jonathan Swift. Appointed Principal Painter to George I in 1723.

CORNELIUS JONSON (1593-1661/2) Leading portrait painter, born in England of German and Flemish extraction. Returned to The Netherlands in early stages of the Civil War. His works are mainly portrait busts, sometimes three-quarter lengths. The full-length at Boughton is quite rare.

SIR GODFREY KNELLER (1646/9-1723) Born Lubeck. Trained by a student of Rembrandt and possibly Rembrandt himself. Spent time in Italy, arrived in England 1676, and became the leading portrait painter of his day. Knighted in 1692, his Academy founded in 1711 was the first in England. Employed many assistants and several hundred portraits documented and signed resulted. Some run-of-the-mill paintings but at his best is free and full of character. Half a dozen portraits by him at Boughton with several others attributed to his school or followers.

SIR PETER LELY (1618-80) Came to London from Haarlem in about 1641, worked with William Dobson, and influenced by Van Dyck, he was a major force in portraiture, particularly after the Restoration. Developed the 'portrait in a landscape', a type popular until the latter 18th century. Created for himself a great collection, its sale after his death being referred to as 'the first of the spectacular picture auctions of the modern world'. Ralph Montagu purchased the Van Dyck grisailles from it. Boughton has 4 definite portraits by Lely with another 8 attributed to him.

SEBASTIANO MAINARDI (1455-1513) Italian. pupil and brother-in-law of Ghirlandaio and long time assistant.

ANTON RAPHAEL MENGS (1728-79) Son of the Dresden Court painter, was greatly influenced by observations of classical sites including Herculaneum. Painted ceiling at Rome's Villa Albani one of his best known works. Travelled back-and-forth between there and the Court in Madrid. A precursor of the Neoclassicism of Jacques Louis David. Also a good portrait painter.

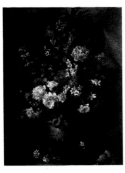

JEAN BAPTISTE MONNOYER (1634-99) French flower painter celebrated for the richness and detail of his work. Brought to London about 1678 by Ralph Montagu for whom he worked extensively at Montagu House and Ditton, where many of the paintings by him at Boughton originated. Made fashionable by Ralph, he is often known simply as 'Baptiste'.

BARTOLOMÉ ESTEBAN MURILLO (1618-82) Spanish. Leading painter from Seville, well known for his devotional works and sometimes sentimental figures. Fine portrait painter. Vaporous style of Murillo's later years is also the period of the Boughton 'Infant St. John in the Wilderness' (c. 1670).

GIOVANNI FRANCESCO PENNI (1496-1528) Italian. Born in Florence but working mostly in Rome, Penni was an assistant – with Guilio Romano – to Raphael, and they continued to work on collaborative projects after their master's death. Penni died in Naples.

SAMUEL SCOTT (1702-72) English marine and topographical painter, the latter influenced by Canaletto with whom he worked when latter was in London.

HUBERT LE SUEUR (active 1610-43) Sculptor, who came to England from France in 1629, worked for Charles I and did a number of tombs in Westminster Abbey.

EUSTACHE LE SUEUR (1616-55) French. Taught by Simon Vouet, influenced by his contemporary, Poussin, and then Raphael. Combined delicate sentiment with a severe classicism.

DAVID TENIERS THE YOUNGER (1610-90) Flemish, Became a Master in Antwerp in 1632 and stayed for twenty years before becoming Court Painter in Brussels to Archduke Leopold Wilhelm, Regent of the Netherlands. Prolific and varied output includes landscapes and genre scenes. Teniers travelled to England between 1650-55, buying pictures sold off by the Commonwealth from Charles I's collection. After 1662 many of his pictures incorporate background views of the château of The Three Towers near Perck, bought from the second husband of Hélène Fourment, widow of Rubens. The Boughton piece is evidently among them.

JOHN WOOTTON (1682-1764) One of the first English landscape painters to be influenced by Claude and Gaspar Poussin.

FRANCESCO ZUCCARELLI (1702-88) Florentine born painter who worked mainly in Venice before going to England in 1752. Founder member of the Royal Academy, appears in the Royal Collection and was popular for the light and decorative touch of his landscapes and figures.

# FURNITURE AND DECORATIVE ARTS

JOSEPH BAUMHAUER (d. 1772) German. Came to Paris in 1740s, married a French cabinet-maker's daughter. Dealer and cabinet-maker to King Louis XV by 1749. His writing table at Boughton with Sèvres plaques dated 1758 is one of the very earliest to use this form of decoration on furniture.

ANDRÉ-CHARLES BOULLE (1642-1732) French creator of wonderful furniture during the reign of Louis XIV and the man who gave his name to a generic style of metal work and tortoiseshell marquetry that found renewed popularity in the late 18th and 19th centuries. Began work in 1672 when admitted to the studios of the Louvre, the Ecole du Roi for artists and decorators which was later transferred to Versailles. The decorative element of 'Boulle work' often consists of tortoiseshell (shell of a turtle, boiled until soft, sometimes backed with red or blue colouring) mixed with brass and pewter cut out in elaborate scrolling designs, at times embellished with mother of pearl and ebony. Boulle had a large manufacturing enterprise but, both at Boughton and elsewhere in The Buccleuch Collection, there are a number of pieces which can be attributed directly to him and which show his influence not just on surface decoration but on form and shape, the elegant writing table in the Rainbow Room being one.

MARTIN CARLIN (1730-85) b. Freiburg, moved to Paris, working for J-F Oeben, whose sister he married in 1759. The small writing table, or bonheur-du-jour in the drawing room with Sèvres plaques (dated 1768) was commissioned by S-P Poirier possibly for Mme du Barry. It shows a considerable advance in the use of porcelain compared with the Joseph Baumhauer writing desk ordered by the same Parisian dealer ten years before.

PIERRE GOLE (1620-84) Dutch. Moved, about 1643, to Paris, eventually taking over the studio of Adrien Garbrant. Became involved in Louis

XIV's Manufacture Royale des Gobelins after 1660 and the King's move to Versailles. Precursor to Boulle whose importance in developing the techniques of wooden and metal marquetry is increasingly recognised.

BENJAMIN GOODISON (1700-67) furniture maker first identified working in 1719 at Blenheim. Major figure in dissemination of style of William Kent, particularly associated with furniture of an architectural character. Re-framed some of the Monnoyer flower paintings for the 2nd Duke.

 GERRIT JENSEN (active 1680-1715) Often referred to as the 'English Boulle', though he was more indebted to Pierre Gole. Became liveryman in the Joiners' Company of London in 1685. As seen at Boughton was very versatile in use of materials and styles.

WILLIAM KENT (1685-1748) b. in Yorkshire, trained as a painter but as his career evolved to designer and decorator, gardener and architect became crucial figure in the development the Palladian style in England. Worked with Lord Burlington at Chiswick House and Lord Leicester on Holkham and many others including Houghton. Huge influence on decoration and design seen indirectly at Boughton in giltwood mirrors, console tables and picture frames.

 PIERRE LANGLOIS (d.1765) French immigrant ébéniste who established a thriving cabinet-making business thanks to trade embargoes imposed during the Seven Years War; his workshops in Tottenham Court Road specialised in inlaid marquetry tops.

ETIENNE LEVASSUEUR (1721-98) Worked with one of Boulle's sons, patronised by Louis XV, became a Master in 1767, developing Neoclassical Louis XVI style.

DANIEL MAROT (1661-1752) Described by the late John Cornforth as the eminence grise of English interiors in the 1690s and 1700s. A Huguenot refugee who fled France to Holland after the revocation of the Edict of Nantes (1685) where he worked at Het Loo for William of Orange. Came to England with the King and is known to have worked at Hampton Court. By then, a pure designer rather than himself the craftsman or architect, the various volumes of prints that survive show his enormous influence an all aspects of interior decoration of the William and Mary period. Drawings of his can be closely linked to the appearance of the North Front of Boughton, his name is found in the margins of Ralph Montagu's surviving account books, and his connection with the Duke is confirmed in various decorative panels at Boughton which are clearly to his design. In many ways the guiding spirit behind both Boughton and Montagu House.

JAMES MOORE THE ELDER (1670-1726)  Cabinet maker with son of same name who became one of the most important furniture suppliers particularly in the 1720s. Did some work with William Kent. As seen in chest and tables at Boughton one of Moore's skills was in gilt-gesso work where the gesso was built up in layers on a wood ground, carved in low relief and gilded.

JOHN VANDERBANK French Huguenot tapestry weaver working at the Great Wardrobe in London with the title of Yeoman Arrasmaker from 1689-1717. Inventive in designing his tapestries to accommodate changing tastes, in particular highly popular chinoiserie panels. As well as various bacchanalian scenes at Boughton, he undertook the magnificent Elements series taken from designs by Charles Le Brun.

# GLOSSARY

BOMBÉ French word used to describe a chest with swelling, convex facade. A popular style of the Regency period of early eighteenth century France.

BONHEUR-DU-JOUR The name given in France, during the eighteenth century, to any small writing desk for a lady. The drawers for such desks rested at the back of the writing surface in a tiered format.

BUREAU PLAT A flat-topped and wide writing desk with only a single drawer; this was contained within the horizontal strip (frieze) that supported the table top, where one would be seated.

BROCADE A heavy silk, cotton or woollen fabric with a raised design, often in metallic thread.

DAMASK Rich woven, silk, linen or cotton fabric with a satin weave.

ÉBÉNISTE Literally 'woodworker' in French and deriving from the word ebony. These 'workers' specialized in veneered furniture.

EBONIZED Wood stained black to mimic ebony. It was popularized in the eighteenth and nineteenth centuries.

GESSO Combination of plaster of Paris, linseed oil and glue, it was used as a base upon ornamental furniture, and could be carved and then gilded.

GRISAILLE Painting in grey tones, sometimes to simulate relief work.

GOTHIC REVIVAL (alt. Gothik) Movement spanning mid-eighteenth to the mid-nineteenth centuries, it sought to draw attention, initially, to medieval building decorative styles.

ISFAHAN Central region of, now, modern-day Iran – formerly Persia.

JAPANNED Decorative technique from the seventeenth century, which attempts to imitate genuine oriental lacquer.

MARQUETRY Shaped pieces of wood, brass ('Boulle marquetry') or pewter etc of differing colours combine, jig-sawlike, to form a veneered pattern or picture. The technique emanates from the Low Countries from of sixteenth century.

MONOGRAM Graphic symbol consisting of two or more letters (initials) combined.

NEOCLASSICAL A counter-Rococo style beginning in the late eighteenth-century that specified a revived interest in ancient Greece and Rome. Geometric shapes and patterns from the birth of civilization were very much in vogue.

PREMIÈRE-PARTIE and CONTRE-PARTIE A term associated with marquetry whereby the design, delicately cut from a sheet of, generally, brass is often inlaid into a tortoiseshell background.

TORCHÈRES French for a lamp or candlestand consisting of a small-topped table, a supporting column linking the legs and top.

TROMPE L'OEIL Literally, in French, 'trick of the eye.' Work described with this characteristic would often mimic in 2-dimensions the tangible qualities of non-existent objects particular to their context. Therefore the detailed reproduction of an urn would also depict the shadow it would cast in relation to the direction any physical light might emanate from.

# THE BOUGHTON LANDSCAPE

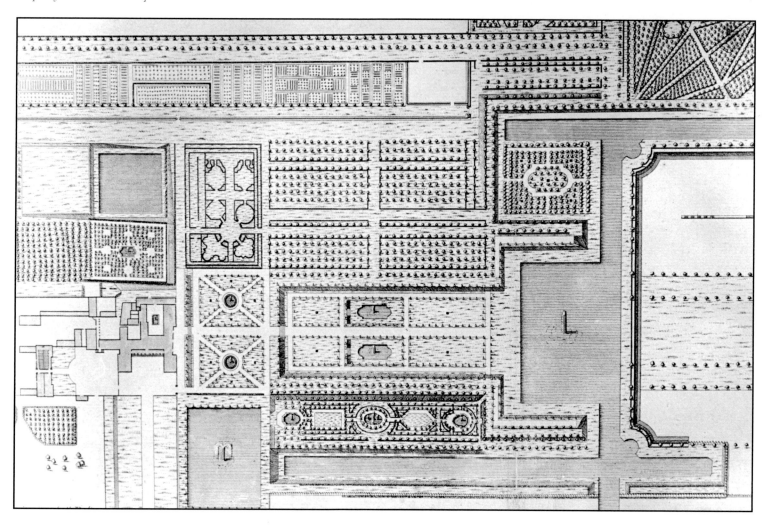

Even before Ralph Montagu got to work on building the North Front, he had engaged a Dutchman called Van der Meulen to begin creating the most magnificent garden setting for his newly enlarged house.

Familiar as Montagu was with Versailles and St Cloud, it is no surprise to find elaborate parterres, water basins and fountains featuring strongly in the designs, with lengthy runs of canal that were essentially Dutch in origin.

The scale of the work was considerable – perhaps even over-ambitious. It took place inside a walled deer park that was first enclosed in the 1470s but had been enlarged by successive Montagus to over 700 acres. In a letter in 1694 Charles Hatton wrote: '*Here is great talk of vast gardens at Boughton but I heard my Lord Montagu is very much concerned that ye water with which he had hoped to make so fine fountains hath failed his expectations.*'

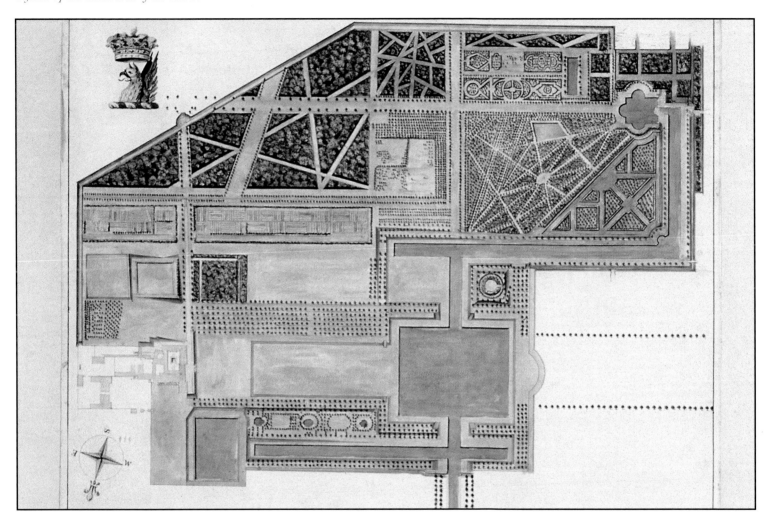

*1746 Watercolour plan of the Gardens by Brazier and Reffield. The House is to the left, the lake is its present size, and the mound is top right above it and defined by the intersection of the canals.*

Early plans show at least a dozen pools and fountains to the west of the House, in addition to the elaborate cascade at the south end, where the River Ise flowed back to its natural course.

A combination of changing taste and the sheer expense of such garden styles led to the more extensive form of landscaping evolved by Duke John. The 1722 plan in *Vitruvius Britannicus* shows already underway a process that, by the time of the 1746 watercolour, had seen most of the parterres grassed over and the Broadwater much extended to the size we see today. A mound was created in one of the right angles of the canals, possibly for the construction of a mausoleum, although initially for a circle of trees, as can be seen in the bird's eye view attributed to Charles Bridgeman and illustrated on p.44.

Above all, John was a planter of avenues, elms, which have sadly now gone, and grand old limes, many of which still stretch across the countryside.

The benign neglect into which the
House fell for the remainder of the 18th
and 19th centuries was equally beneficial
for the landscape.

The bones survive, albeit hidden, and it
is now undergoing a major restoration
programme, embarked on almost thirty
years ago when the present Duke had
the Broadwater dug out. Hundreds of
avenue trees are being replanted, using,
where possible, clones of the distinctive
limes associated with Boughton; fences,
walls and gates are being renewed; and
most recently the 'Dead Reach' arm of
the water system has been re-dug – a
prelude to refilling the 'Grand Etang'
whose basin can be clearly seen outside
the North Front. It is a programme that
will take a decade or more to complete,
and many more thereafter to mature, but
one day future generations will benefit in
the way we do from what our forebears
did 300 years ago.

*The Dead Reach shortly after
restoration in 2005/6*

# THE MONTAGU MONUMENTS IN THE VILLAGE CHURCHES

Most of the Montagu tombs and monuments can be found in churches in two of the villages adjoining the Estate. The earlier ones are in Weekley, the later ones in Warkton. The churches are not generally open but visits can be made by prior appointment, through the Church Wardens.

Saint Edmund's Church in the village of Warkton, just to the south, is distinguished by its chancel, which was built shortly after 1749 and contains an exceptional grouping of four large memorials to the three later generations of the Montagu family.

The first two are of John, 2nd Duke and his widow Mary who survived him by two years. Both monuments are by Louis François Roubiliac (c. 1705-62). Born in Lyon, Roubiliac had settled in England by 1735 and produced many memorials in Westminster Abbey.

The next statue is of their daughter Mary Montagu, wife of George Brudenell, 3rd Duke of Montagu. Designed by Robert Adam (1728-92), the Scottish architect, with sculpture by Peter Mathias van Gelder (active in London in the 1770s), it was erected in 1781.

The final monument is to the memory of her daughter, Elizabeth, Duchess of Buccleuch and Queensberry, who died in 1827 aged 83. She was the last of the Montagus of Boughton. The striking statue was designed and sculpted by Thomas Campbell.

*Weekley Church*

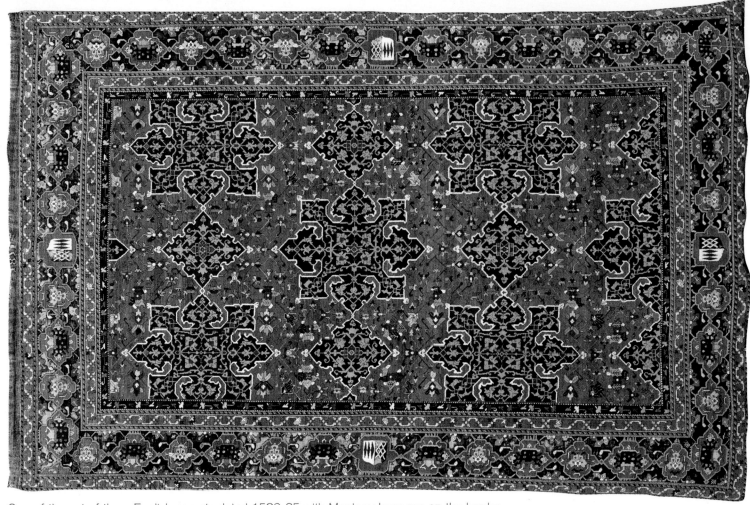

One of the set of three English carpets dated 1583-85 with Montagu lozenges on the border.

Text by The Earl of Dalkeith, KBE
Gareth Fitzpatrick, Charles Lister, Mark Adams

Creative Advice from Lord and Lady John Scott.

Design by Nick McCann
Technical Supervision by Matthew Limbert

Photography by The Duke of Buccleuch, KT, The Earl of Dalkeith, KBE,
John Beedle, Michael Crick, John Edwards, Gareth Fitzpatrick, Valerie Finnis,
Lance Goffort-Hall, Jeanette Hill, David Hope, Alex Jolly, Moira Leggat,
Nick McCann, Cameron Manson, Manuela Schellermann, Fritz von der Schulenberg

Architectural drawing of the development of Boughton House
on page 18 by Elizabeth Hampson

Architectural drawing of the State Rooms page 30 courtesy of
English Heritage (Monuments), RCHME, Crown Copyright

Published by Heritage House Group Limited
Heritage House, Lodge Lane, Derby DE1 3HE
Tel: 01332 347087 Fax: 01332 290688
Email: publications@hhgroup.co.uk

For further information on Boughton House see

"Boughton House – The English Versailles"
Edited by Tessa Murdoch

The website **www.boughtonhouse.org.uk** has further illustrations of
the House, the Collection and the work of The Living Landscape Trust,
and contact details and opening arrangements of the other
Buccleuch Historic Houses.

The Living Landscape Trust is an educational charity established in 1986 to
administer Boughton House, the Collection and the educational access.

The Living Landscape Trust
Boughton House
Kettering, Northamptonshire
England, NN14 1BJ
Telephone: 01536 515731 Fax: 01536 417255
Email: llt@boughtonhouse.org.uk